CHAMPION

21st Century Women
Guardians of Wealth & Legacy

Leslie Thomas Flowers

A Special Bonus from Leslie

Now that you have your copy of Champion. 21st Century Women: Guardians of Wealth & Legacy, you are on your way to earning more in business and being a Champion in your life and that of your clients, colleagues, families and friends.

You also receive the special bonus I created to add to your personal and professional growth; something you can use starting today. This journal allows you to study new ways of thinking and apply what you learn, reflect, and note insights about navigating through today's economy as a women doing business in the 21st century.

The perfect complement to Champion, claim your copy here.

http://leslie-flowers.com/ChampionJournal

The sooner you begin learning the things you may not know, the sooner you are on your way to success in business and happiness all around.

Leslie

This book is dedicated to the Champion woman — courageous enough to step out and speak for those who have not yet found their voice — and stand for their greatness.

And to Brooke, Sydney, Julia, and Blake who are guardians of my legacy, now and into the next century.

Acknowledgments

I'd like to acknowledge J. 'Ross' Cornwell, the first editor of the Napoleon Hill Foundation newsletter and editor of the go-to version used worldwide of Napoleon Hill's classic *Think and Grow Rich! The Original Version, Restored and Revised ™* for being *my* champion in understanding and navigating the often bumpy world of personal development, publishing, and application of Napoleon Hill's work. You are the rudder every ship needs when coursing from point A to point B.

As well I am acknowledging my friend, colleague, mastermind accountability partner, and confidante, Diana M. Needham, who never once let me lose sight of my own greatness in the making. While Ross was my rudder, Diana handled both oars, sometimes at the same time, to ensure I didn't capsize in this effort.

Preface

YOU NEVER GIVE UP!

That would be an apt subtitle for Leslie Thomas Flowers's newest work – Champion. 21st Century Women: Guardians of Wealth & Legacy.

Leslie has achieved something extraordinary with this book. She has taken the up and down events and circumstances of her life and produced from them a road map, a step-by-step blueprint for today's women struggling to achieve success in business and in life.

The keystone of her teaching is that while what you know is important, what you do with what you know is paramount. "Purpose" is vital, but purpose without thought, and thought without action are fruitless. What she teaches in the way of practical steps you must take to achieve directed action in your life is a lesson of inestimable value.

Do yourself a favor. Get copies of Champion for yourself, women who are family, friends, and associates, and, yes, even those males you know who could use an "achievement boost" to get ahead. You won't regret it. Neither will they.

Ross Cornwell
Compiler and editor of the upcoming new edition of
Think and Grow Rich!: The Original Version, Restored and Revised

Introduction

Why I wrote this book

At the turn of this Century, I sat in the dark for two years in the home I loved so well, in which I raised my two children over two decades. Now, overnight, it became my tomb, a place to give up and die, and I wore a constant veil that let in no light. I went to work every day, came home, and cried. One day my 30 year marriage was alive and thriving; the next it was dead - dead as a doornail.

What happened 'overnight' was a complete devastation and end of the life I had been living happily for as long as I could remember. I was heartbroken when my parents died at early ages of course. This however was the implosion of my 'American dream.' When I walked through my home I was walking over earthquake rubble; with no sure footing as my roots had been cut to the quick.

I did some crazy things ... things when I look at now ... I'd rather not look at all, to 'stop the change that was inevitable.' My American dream of marriage was about never giving up. I was proud we had made it 30 years in the face of divorce now the norm. That meant sticking with it no matter what. It meant keeping my word; the word I had given before God, family and friends. It meant doing 'whatever it took' to maintain that family unit. Eventually however the writing was on the wall.

I was 55. Both children were on their own. All retirement money and property vanished. You see while I was working and 'healing,' my husband and I lived in different domiciles. He had been *'investing'* all our life savings without my knowledge. The investments yielded nothing and I walked away after thirty years with $4000 in my pocket.

Like you eventually I picked myself up by the bootstraps and began living life again. The veil almost never showed up now as a reminder ... and life was good again.

Coming home from work one Friday afternoon, I grabbed the mail and looked at it in the car. There was a letter from the IRS. I opened it and what I read threw me for a loop. The instructions were to include my first monthly payment of $5000 to pay back $80,000 I owed!

I was a secretary earning about $3000 clear a month at that time. There was no way! How did this happen?

The way I saw it I had three choices. One was to throw in the towel, sell everything, and live on the street. Second was to let them take me to jail. Third was drive off a bridge.

This was wrong. I knew this wasn't my doing but does it matter who is responsible when it comes to owing the government?

Then I remembered I had $500 stashed away in an Edward Jones account and I knew the broker well. I called him and went in the next day and told him what happened.

What he said changed the course of my life. I didn't know it then ... I had simply *sought 'specialized knowledge'* (expert advice) which I learned later is a critical element in applying the principles of success for achievement -- in business and in life. He told me I needed a tax attorney who is also a CPA ... and he had a recommendation.

Eighteen months later and $5000 paid to the attorney, $50k of the $80k was removed from my debt. Quiet when the attorney told me we had done well, he asked in a very uncomfortable 'pregnant' pause, if I wanted to appeal. Yes, I said. Twelve months and $1800 later, the entire $80k was removed from my debt.

My credit was in the toilet of course, but I was coming out of this too!

This is a woman who lived a colorful life. College in San Francisco, flight attendant shuttling US troops into and out of Viet Nam in the 60's (with overnights in Hawaii, Philippines and Japan), danced Flamenco, studied humanities at San Francisco State and played in a rock band. Nothing ever stopped me. I was always moving forward, moving forward.

One day after picking up the mail ... oh, no ... a letter from the State department of revenue this time! Dear Mrs. Flowers .... you owe us $20,000! And here's your payment book, etc., etc. When I told the State staff member in charge the decision of the IRS, they waived that $20,000 as well as so I was debt free!

I wrote this book so YOU NEVER GIVE UP no matter how tough your plight may seem. I had lead a charmed life and was grateful for it. I never thought all this would happen. It did and it does and the next dozen years I spent transforming and reshaping what I knew to be true up until that day so many years ago.

Over the years I have honed my skills as a teacher, a writer, a mentor, a friend, and a champion to women that DO NOT GIVE UP when they know their inner truth.

We are never given an idea we cannot do. I had the idea, pursued it, and it all worked out. My choices, had I not made that call to my 'financial rep,' were dismal and not for this woman. This woman who raised two amazing children; who was a good wife; who served her community year after year ... all of this ... this was NOT the end for me!

During those years I sat in the dark and then dealt with the government, I had my eye on a home on a small lake not far from where I was living. When it came on the market I was unable to purchase it because of my credit score. It was 5 years later when it came back on the market; my score passed and I bought it. I bought it in 2009 at $100k less than it sold for two years before -- my first home purchase on my own and I was over 60. I visualized myself over those years until I bought it, living *in* the home. All the rooms face the lake and the wrap around deck allows me to be part of the eco culture. It was a dream home.

The next years were all about learning and teaching, and personal development. Already well trained as a coach, I began to look at more and more disciplines, each one making me more aware of my true and infinite potential. I studied transformation, leadership, quantum physics, metaphysics, mind control, spirituality, Abraham-Hicks, the Enneagram ... just about all of it. I was FULL of knowledge and proof that this all worked. Now to figure out a way to do what I loved and make money too. The 'now' in this sentence came after buying books and programs ... many more than I ever read or applied. There was something in the 'gathering' of the material and the 'throwing of money' at things that didn't want to stop. So STOPPING spending and running around taking workshops and seminars and filling other people's pockets ... and thinking about my own legacy and how all I had learned could help women be the role models for our children and grand children and be the guardians of wealth and legacy.

In 2008 I landed on the work of Napoleon Hill and his best seller Think and Grow Rich. For the next 5 years solid I studied and facilitated dozens of face to face weekly mastermind studies with 6 to 12 people per study digging deeply into this classic. Some studies I did concurrently and they were not on the same chapter. I was working 30 hours a week so the mastermind studies I did initially at no charge and then a modest amount. All great until I retired and had to play for REAL.

I noticed many of my clients had businesses but were like me. They had a backup plan ... a husband or a retirement fund ... something so running a real business was not a priority.

People studying Hill's work with me were lit up with the principles of success. Most clients were women. We really do thrive when we are learning. It really is the 'miracle grow' of life for humans. But why I thought, was I so immersed in this crotchety male content written almost 100 years ago?

My answer came when I attended a luncheon when the results of a report done for our State by the IWPR (Institute of Women's Policy Research) revealed something so staggering, it caught my attention like a tuning fork. This was it: **women in our state earn 17.5% less than men ... and ... it would not be until 2054 when the gap collapse on its own based on current statistics.**

During that luncheon I got a hunch ... or an intuitive 'hit' right in my chest. HERE was my answer! The WHY! I was now uniquely qualified to teach these timeless complex concepts ... women were completely unaware of them. Not a clue about the principles of success developed and used by men for more than 200 centuries.

I then spent several years translating the principles and my own teaching platform into a language women can embrace creating a unique, achievement driven mastermind program, to first overcome fear by mustering enough courage to do what it takes to earn what they should. Then build their businesses to a point of predicting a consistent and upward monthly income, reaping the byproduct of more confidence in business. I will explain why this does not happen for women ... they are rarely able to gain traction and momentum in their businesses.

This quarterly women's mastermind program has been facilitated five times with women who have stayed in the program and can now measure palpable results ... business results by momentum and upward swing in revenue generation ... and personal results ... a new knowing of our ability and inherent greatness that is what many refer to as confidence.

I wrote this book so you have a roadmap; a blueprint; a plan to begin. Until thought is linked with purpose, there is no intelligent accomplishment.[1] No matter how smart I was, or how much action I was taking, it was not until I understood it was useless until I could create a plan or goal or intention or purpose with the outcome being achieved every time. It's a formula that is tried and true now and I want you to know what is available as a result of my years of work in personal development.

If this book has you stop and move into your purpose and developing your legacy, it's been worth it.

If this book reveals truths you already knew yet now in a new clear way and it motivates you into action ... well that of course is the purpose of a goal! To get you into directed action.

So I wrote this book to help women who are already know a level of success, and want more to get their message out to the world. They aren't worried about getting into action; they're in action. They want direction. And they want a Champion.

For whom the book is written

This book is written for the woman who is already on your way to greatness. You've had a taste of it already. You are already a success. You are already confident. Perhaps you are as I was, very much in a "fire, aim, ready" mode -- already in motion, at bat, and swinging at the next pitch. Swinging and spinning like a whirligig.

You will have a good idea if this book is right for you if you know you are already on your path yet are clear there is more to know. More to reshape the "fire, aim, ready" mindset to change it to one of "ready, aim, then fire." You know that's more effective. You may not however be managing it yet.

---

[1] James Allen, As a Man Thinketh

You are a woman looking for your next step to expand your success, to grow your business further, to predict financial outcomes with regularity, to source and embrace momentum ... because of one thing that is likely the thing that brings you to tears ... your Legacy. What will you leave behind? What will be written about you after you are gone? Imagine it's 150 years from now ... what did you leave behind? You are a woman who knows her purpose and she has a message to get out in the world in a 'big way.'

You are clear that learning has a direct impact on earnings. You've proven that yourself so you are always pursuing new ways of thinking and doing. You know you have a purpose that will serve mankind and you are on fire to share it.

You have had life altering events, some monstrous, and come through them with flair. Never mind how long it may have taken you. In fact you are a woman who knows instinctively by now that for every down there is a matching 'up' and you are in a place of 'expecting' the 'up' to *show up* almost any day. And while you may be impatient, you still keep walking. You are *firing* all over the place and want to see what's next, to put things in order.

You are open to adding new information to your tool belt of skills and are intentional about finding your next step. That's what you really want. You want to see the starting line and the map all the way around the track. You are however okay when I tell you I will only provide the first 50 yards of how-to's even though I know them all.

You are bombarded with all sorts of 'blueprints for success' and you likely have an arsenal of books and programs in which you have invested and with which you wish you had done more. You are by no means perfect. You are simply 'in motion' toward a purpose that will change mankind and leave a Legacy of value. I know you.

You are a no-nonsense, do-it-yourself (for the most part), get it done woman. You can do nearly anything ... with directions.

This book is for you, right now, *if* ... you see yourself in all or part of the description above.

You are a Champion if you speak your truth, stand for others, keep your word, and almost blindly infuse yourself with authority and expertise so you can make a difference in the world, one person at a time. You are a Champion if you want your children, grands and descendants to remember you as the most powerful teacher in your family, sharing your wisdom long after you are gone. It takes desire, yes. You must want it, of course. Above all, you must be WILLING to take action on your own behalf by using the one thing you can control, your conscious thoughts, to serve others.

For whom the book is not written.

This book is not for you, right now, if you bristled at all or part of the description of the woman for whom I wrote this book. She looked foreign to you. You simply don't see yourself this way. You could be somewhere in between of course. You get to decide if you are closer to taking this on 'now,' or not now.

It's not for the woman who is swirling -- that is still in the 'fire, fire, fire' mode, buying this program, taking that seminar -- we call that learning ... to a point. How long do you repeat this behavior until you STOP and take action?

This book is not for you if you don't believe you have greatness within you ... not yet, that is. You don't believe you can succeed and you have proof from past failures.

You are sure that people, conditions and circumstances are responsible for your lot in life -- particularly your inability to be the success you dream of being. You have not yet accepted full responsibility for all of your life ... the way it is, and the way it is not.

If you decide this book is not for you because you match all or some of the attributes I've just mentioned, it's really all right. Our 'inner journey' is just that ... our own, and it takes time. Growing 'conscious awareness' is a process. Not being ready now only means that you will certainly be ready at some point.

What I know for certain is this: You will know when you possess the mindset that is ready for this book because yours matches the description of the woman for whom this book is actually written.

How to use this book.

The information in this book is not to 'replace' what you already know. It is to 'add to' what you know to develop a solid foundation of faith. Faith in yourself and faith in the 'way of the universe.'

Read several paragraphs and pause for a moment to check in to see if the information resonates or 'confuses' you. If it confuses you, skip over it. It will become clear at a later point in time when you read it again.

If you are looking for things you disagree with, that you are sure don't work (you've tried them before) and are unwilling to believe that there actually is a way to expand your business, get your message out, and leave a Legacy, you are not ready for this book right now.

Because we are never given an idea we cannot do, note ideas you get along the way. If any word used musters up an unpleasant feeling in your mid section, this is a good thing. Pause for a moment and jot down what it was. When you revisit it at another time, look to see where this 'trigger' came from. Was it an incident? Do you remember your age?

Then change the word the next time you hear it to one that resonates with you and means the same thing.

Earmark a certain amount of time for reading. Do only that. Mixing reading with other activities will interrupt the flow of your growth in awareness of your own true potential.

Remind yourself that for every up, there is a down. For dark, there is light. For a subjective reaction, there is an equal and opposite objective response. Catching your negative thought is step 1. Shifting it to its polar opposite is the second. Practicing is 3rd. And 4th you will note your shifting your mindset has become a habit ... to look for the positive side of the coin automatically.

Keep in mind this quote by Thoreau, *If one advances confidently in the direction of his dreams, and endeavors to live the life which he has imagined, he will meet with a success unexpected in common hours.*

He is saying that we don't need to LEAP out of the gate; that we can take small steps (as long as we keep moving). And that we try, make an effort, or endeavor to live the life we want. Finally that our success shows up from unexpected sources and at unexpected times.

Table of Contents

Great minds discuss ideas; average minds discuss events; small minds discuss people.

We gain strength, and courage, and confidence by each experience in which we really stop to look fear in the face ... we must do that which we think we cannot.

Happiness is not a goal; it is a by-product.

Eleanor Roosevelt

I. Women, Wealth & Wages

In the late 1990's, with several decades working full time in corporate America under my belt, I was introduced to my new boss at a small scientific company in Research Triangle Park, NC. Serving as desktop publisher (from secretary to technical information specialist) I managed the company's proposal production department. If you were a secretary in the 60's and stayed in the field through century end, you had to go through all iterations of word processing, magnetic card readers, MTST a huge machine with a tape on both sides, and more. Without display with the MTST (magnetic tape selectric typewriter) you would transfer a document from the right tape to the left one having to 'catch' where the changes had to be made in between, on the keyboard. All the way through to the TRS 80 (Tandy Radio Shack) ... the computer that stored information on an 8" floppy disk, smaller floppy discs, floppy discs that were no longer floppy and more. They got small and weren't flexible. You by this time had to be a master of the craft of being a 'secretary.' I say craft as I also learned to write DOS batch files, teach computer aided drafting systems (CADD) to architects, and more.

About five feet three inches tall and dressed in a well fitted pantsuit, my new boss smiled and extended her hand which I took and shook. We talked freely and in a very short time I recognized something very familiar about her. Her conversation included certain words that were 'coined' by a transformational technology -- one which I had studied in great depth over time. When I asked if she had done 'the work,' she said yes, and that "the technology changed her life." The best part was that since we spoke the same language, I could always be straight with her and not worry about being judged or evaluated on a personal level. We both had done Landmark Education programs.

Over the next few months I marveled as I watched her fit right in with all the male directors and c-level executives sans one woman director in statistics. She seemed relaxed and confident no matter what she was doing.

One day as we caught up on activities and I sat across from her in her office, I had been itching to ask her something and because of our relationship at this point, I did. "How do you get along with all the men managers so well?" Her answer changed my entire perspective on women in business and became an important milestone in my career. She said with a smile, *"I do what they do."*

She was right ... she did. I watched her closely from then on and she seemed to interact as they did. They all had short bullet-point dialogues with one another. They shook hands coming and going and they all stood rather still while they talked. I never saw them socializing like their direct reports. They were short, cordial and to the point. And she 'fit in' like a glove.

When I first learned the cold, hard statistics about the gender wage gap — how much more men earn than women for doing the same job, and by when the gap would close — I was in shock. I began to think of my granddaughters and great granddaughters to be, waiting to be paid what they deserve, while being integral in the financial responsibility of their families. I realized there was not only something I could do to crush that gap ... I was fired up about it! I have just the right training, experience and skills to start teaching women what to do to begin crushing and squeezing the life out of the gender wage gap right now.

And if I didn't, then who would? Our mothers and grandmothers ... and theirs ... took their risks on our behalf, stepped out in the face of adversity, and made a difference one woman at a time. It has to be done that way to make steady inroads in more promotions and better pay for women. That is precisely how we crush the gap early and turn the tables in our favor in short order -- stepping out, taking action, and taking a stand! Being a Champion for others.

As you read further, see if any of the behavioral business skills mentioned could be affecting your own opportunities for growth in business. Few women have mastered them all, however. It's about learning, mastering, then *habitualizing* one skill at a time, at your own pace, that ultimately keeps you inspired and engaged, bringing you one step closer to success. You may feel the laughter of recognition swelling in your smile as things begin to get very clear for you ... and you *know* what to do next.

After 45 years in corporate and 20 years in professional development, it was very clear to me that most women are invisible -- not seen or heard by business leaders, both men and women. Being invisible yields lack of credibility. And not being seen or heard gives us almost no opportunity for advancement.

When I held the position of document production supervisor for a company in the healthcare industry, I noticed two small things over the 5 years I worked there.

1. While our department was the last pair of eyes on huge proposals (thousands of pages) that had to arrive picture perfect by a certain time or date (or would end up in the trash), and I ran it effectively, there was no 'step up' for me in the organization -- no place for me to 'go.' No path to director or executive level. I was stuck there or I could choose to leave.

2. Small yet telling ... after securing an 8 figure contract, the company did ample expansion with window offices around the whole floor. Every single person that had direct reports was assigned a window office, except ... you guessed it ... me. I had 4 direct reports

and was not even considered. When I brought this up to my supervisor, I did get the window office. The point here for me was that it wasn't even a 'thought' in anyone's mind. That's invisibility.

During the dot.com era while working for a small tech startup, a coup ensued (not atypical then) during a Board meeting which I attended by phone. When an attendee in the meeting asked about my position, the board member in charge told them all "her services are no longer needed." For about 10 seconds my blood began to boil and then something magical happened. I did a 180 in my thinking and said to myself, "I don't want to be where I am not wanted. I have excellent skills and I want to be working with people who appreciate what I bring to the table."

Figure 1 Whether small business or corporate, women are invisible.

Women are **invisible** in business, therefore **not credible**, and **passed over** for deserved opportunities for advancement.

Isn't it time for you to be visible, credible and enjoy opportunities for advancement? I say YES, it is time!

Were you at all surprised that women are earning far less than men? No? I didn't think so.

It has been this way since I can remember when my mother's part time job for 'pin' or 'mad' money in the late 50's and early 60's, turned into a full time job in the 70's, and by the 80's, *all* her wages were *required* to support the household. Earning less is frustrating for you - - today's working woman. You are challenged to make ends meet, you may well be 'doing it all' on your own, and you live longer, paying more for insurance.

Business success today has its own *personality* .. and you likely guessed that -- it is *male*. It made perfect sense to me when I realized for the past 200 generations or so since we began recording history, that history was recorded and read by men, and then the virtues and timeless principles recorded were practiced by men in business, consistently and repeatedly over time, until *their* way of doing things effectively, simply *set the landscape for success in business.* It became automatic -- a habit.

During that same 200 generations of course women were developing their own unique skills including leadership, collaboration, and peacemaking.

If we had had the luxury of declaring 'in 5 years we'll go into business,' between now and then, we could learn the skills required to be as successful as our male counterparts before we even started! No. We're already in the thick of it. And most of us are like fish out of water in business

I suspect men becoming 'house husbands' while their wives work, experience the *same fish out of water* experience, as their inherent skills are not very useful in successful home management.

Figure 2 Men have set the context for business success through the ages.

Men are unaware of the source of their own influence in business as they are a collection of inherent and hidden habits.

When a habit becomes clear to you -- you 'distinguish' it -- see it in action -- you then have the power to leverage it to influence results, turning the tides in your favor. The awareness offered you in this book will have you begin intentionally directing that leverage so you begin to show up as visible and credible; achieving what you already deserve in business, right away.

I want you to have an understanding of 'how' we got in this fix ... where we are unseen, unheard, and passed over in business.

Note the first law of the universe which is mentioned again in this book is ORDER, and out of confusion comes order. We are tentative when we are not clear yet take quick steps when we are sure.

You do the math, 200+ generations or 5000 Years is more than enough time for those timeless skills to be 'born into' men so they can use them to be successful in business. Use them yet be unaware they have them.

You know this modern business man who has the confidence to step up to the plate yet in so many cases, he does not complete his work on time or as promised. Then watch the female staff come in and 'clean up' for him by completing his tasks. Why? Because we're good at cleaning up a lot of things at once. Business however requires being laser focused on one thing at a time.

Let's take a look at the 100th Monkey Effect or experiment[2] as example and see what it provides.

---

[2] 100th Monkey Effect

Figure 3 100th Monkey Effect

In 1952 Japanese Scientists dropped sweet potatoes in the sand on a remote island inhabited by Japanese Macaque[3] monkeys. The monkeys loved the sweet potatoes! The little ones learned to wash the sand off before eating them in pretty short order. Adult monkeys either learned from the little ones or just ate the potatoes with the sand.

30 Years and 100 generations later, after practicing the 'washing off' skills over time, suddenly baby monkeys were born already skilled in 'washing off the sand!' And even better, monkeys born on other islands also were born with this skill.

Once I revisited this fascinating experiment *... I saw the CAUSE of the Gender Wage Gap and KNEW I had the SOLUTION! This was a pivotal moment in my career.*

The Cause: Men practicing skills for twice as many generations as the monkeys, would ensure future generations of men would be born already having a set of skills for success in business.

---

[3] http://en.wikipedia.org/wiki/Japanese_Macaque

The Solution: Distinguish those automatic and inherent male behavioral skills -- make them simple and clear -- teach them to women to leverage the same influence, play evenly with men, match the male personality in business (while remaining 100% feminine), and be visible and credible. Oh, and because learning them is intentional, you have the leverage the skills to source your own success.

I was on to something big ... a way to funnel all my training and focus it on squelching this gap before predicted (mid 2050's).

I have a vivid imagination and think in colorful pictures. I am inspired by those images and my creative imagination, and have learned that visualization is another 'key' to influencing results in your favor.

When I saw the Cause and Solution, I saw business success as comparable to playing in a sandbox ... a sandbox created over time by men only. They decided (without being aware) its size and grade of sand, the height of the sides, overall dimensions, the quality of lumber, all with skills or tools they 'inherited' to 'play' effectively and successfully in business.

**Figure 4 Business success requires learning skills to play
shoulder to shoulder with men.**

In my mind's eye, I saw women standing outside the sandbox, with maybe a shovel in hand -- ONE tool! Then I remembered the excitement selling lemonade as a child in front of our house on hot days. Now I could see a stand where the 3 Secrets (the tools) were for sale. All you have to do to play in the sandbox successfully was to step right up and get those skills!

I have identified about a dozen male skills, habits or behaviors that consistently, over time, result in business success. I'm betting you already have some of them! Most of us do ... we just are not 'aware' of the skill so cannot leverage it in our favor. Not yet that is.

And for those skills that you know you have, you will 'see' them clearly now and be able to *use* them starting now to make changes and influence outcomes in your life and turn the tables on the gender wage gap!

So here's what this information can mean to you ... ***A lemonade stand of business success skills for the asking!*** Once you have one or more of them, you can step into the sandbox and play shoulder to shoulder with men. You do have to take some action, yet I bet you'll find it fun! I did and still do!

As you make a skill a habit (you don't even have to think about it anymore), you will be 'matching' the landscape, or playing with all the tools, and you will begin to notice you are 'being listened to!' People start paying attention to what you have to say! Then you know you are making inroads in crushing the gender wage gap ... for yourself, your granddaughters, and your great granddaughters.

Here's an example of women not *being listened to* (and therefore not credible and void of opportunity). See if you find yourself shaking your head yes and smiling.

*You are in a meeting. You say something. Someone else says something. And then someone else. Then a man says **exactly what you said**, and you hear from the others "great idea ... let's do that!!" And you say to yourself wondering if you are crazy ... "didn't I just say those exact words?"*

You are not being listened to by business leaders while not intentional on their part. They are simply operating automatically. If you don't match what they 'know' as business success, they simply stop listening.

The way to navigate through the *3 Secrets System* to modify thoughts and behavior for business is to know that you **only pick one skill to adopt on at a time**! You don't have to do them all at once! And you don't have to pick the one you see as the hardest. Pick one that you know you can make your own very quickly. Consider you probably have some of these skills nailed.

The more skills you take on and make your own, one by one -- the better your shot at success! It doesn't matter which behavior you begin to capture ... *you just have to start.*

The 3 Secrets System allow you to *match* your behavior to the current business landscape, while remaining 100% feminine. You give up nothing. You gain leverage to influence your own results, and turn the tables on the gender wage applecart!

The 3 Secret System

BEHAVIOR, BELIEF & BODY LANGUAGE

Secret 1: Behavior (Self Management)

How do men converse in business?
Men speak in bullet points. They cut to the chase.

How do women converse in business?
Women are narrators. We have to tell the whole story!

Do you tell the whole story? And you feel strongly that every tiny details is required for another to understand? If you are a narrator, would you match the landscape for success? What one thing could you do about it right now?

If you do speak in bullet points, when you see a colleague lose the audience due to saying so much more than is required, what action could you take in service to this woman?

Track your observations below.

ACTION ITEM:

Think about a time when you noticed yourself (or female colleague) 'telling the whole story' and the men began to quickly lose interest. Maybe they rolled their eyes, began checking their cell phones, or were fidgeting. Note your insights.

____

____

____

____

Secret 2(a): Belief (Self Worth)

Do men expect to get that raise or promotion?
Not only do they expect it, they are looking for it.

Do women expect they will get a raise or promotion?
Women do not set the intention or expect to be successful.

If you are not setting an expectation to get promotions, could that me a way you could match yourself to the context for business success? What one thing could you do to begin to expect the raise you deserve?

ACTION ITEM:

Think about a time when you observed a man bragging that he was going to get that promotion or raise in front of everyone. What was your immediate reaction?

Track your observations

NOTE: Think about a time when a female colleague got a deserved promotion. Did you cheer her on? Or did you feel a touch of jealousy?

____

____

____

____

Secret 2(b) : Belief (Self Worth)

Are men confident about their abilities in business?
Men are inherently comfortable and confident in business.

Are women confident about their abilities in business?
Women are like fish out of water and are not yet comfortable in business.

If you are not confident in business you might feel uncomfortable. What action might you take to 'feel' more confident? Even wearing a jacket can start your confidence growing. Secret 2 is the pinnacle of the 3 Secrets. Master it, and you've set your own course!

ACTION ITEM:

Think about a time when you observed a woman walk into a meeting and you instantly knew she was timid. You could just 'tell.' How could you tell? What were the signs?

____

____

____

____

Secret 3(a): Body Language (Perceived Presence)

How do men greet one another in business settings?
Men shake hands when greeting others.

How do women greet one another in business settings?
Women hug.

If you are hugging when greeting, would you show up differently if you chose to shake hands instead? Would you then match the business landscape for success?

ACTION ITEM: In mixed business company.

1. If you are a hugger, would it be hard for you to resist the urge to hug and extend your hand instead? There is nothing wrong with any of your behavior ... it may just not *match* the business landscape of success.
2. If you are a hand-shaker, were you always that way? Or is it a learned behavior? How do you think you learned it?
3. If you do both, what positive result might you get from adopting handshakes only?

____

____

____

____

Secret 3(b): Body Language (Perceived Presence)

How do men stand when doing business?
How do men sit when doing business?

Men stand with feet shoulder width apart, hands at their sides.
Men sit straight without much movement

How do women stand when doing business?
How do women sit when doing business?

Women cross their ankles, put hands on hips and shift weight often.

Women cross their legs and in some cases pull out a mirror to check themselves.

Have you noticed if you fidget in business? If you do, what one thing could you do to be more calm? If you are moving about, changing positions or taking care of personal hygiene when doing business, you do not match the current business landscape for success.

ACTION ITEM:

Do you know yourself to fidget in meetings? What could you do to slow that down right now? Track your observations on the next page.

NOTE: Could wearing lots of noisy jewelry be a mismatch to the context of business success?

____

____

____

____

The 3 Secret System helps you change the 'listening' of business leaders by simply mirroring and matching the behavioral context for success.

Matching the behaviors of business success requires that you take action. Nothing changes until that happens! Pick a skill and follow the steps below to 'own it!'

Why is it so important for men to get onboard with bringing women into full view, seeing them, listening and learning from them, and promoting them?

The top and bottom line for business must improve when adding peacemaking, leadership and collaborative skills to those skills and strengths brought to the table by men.

Figure 5 Improved ROI when skills from men and women are available in business. Visibility, credibility, opportunity for all!

My intention in this chapter is to give you enough information to inspire you to make internal changes for yourself. If you have direct reports, you also have an insight about how they are treated and it will become clear how you can be a Champion for them.

The 3 Secret Process to turn the tables and crush the gender wage gap now!

1. Select one behavioral skill you want to become a habit; write it in a journal.
2. Observe how that skill shows up for men and women in the workplace; your social proof.
3. Mirror or copy the skill you want to improve in your mind; see yourself doing it.
4. Practice it several times publicly and note your results on paper with the date.
5. You make the skill a habit by repeating the practice of that skill consistently over time.
6. You know it's your habit when you are using the skill automatically, without thinking about it anymore.
7. Pat yourself on the back ... and start another skill!

This system is not about controlling outside circumstances. No one can do that. It's about influencing them and turning the tables in your favor! Now watch yourself grow and thrive ... starting right NOW!!

II. Women, Wealth & Self-Assessment

Before you can set a course, you must know where you are to start. There are no right or wrong results in self assessment. It's a starting point only.

In the simple list below, there are optimum ways of 'being' as a Champion and 'less than optimum' ways of being. It is not possible to be at one point on the scale and remain there. We are either growing or slipping back (Law of Motion).

On a scale of 1 - 10 ... 10 being the best you can be, take a look at where you are on your journey right now. Then consider where you want to grow in these areas.

Do you set sail toward what you want with only a crew and a ship, not knowing exactly how you will get there (no map), yet motivated into action? Or do you wait until you know the exact course, how long it will take, how much money you will need, etc.?

Champions do not wait for all the steps. They are good with a couple and will step into the dark and into their fears because they know that it is not until you are in action that the next steps will be revealed to you. And they have seen this before ... how they have to be 'already on their way' to know the next step.

Do you focus on HOW you will accomplish the goal? Or do you pay attention to WHY you want it?

No one can hold more than one 'conscious thought' at a time. You can close your eyes and think of the front door of your home -- the color, scratches, overgrown bushes as example. When your mind shifts to your car, the image of the door disappears and the car pops up in your mind's eye. When we focus on HOW we will do it, we butt-out our WHY. It is the WHY that motivates us ... it is the HOW that stops us.

Do you stand for what is right in the face of adversity? Or do you keep quiet so you don't rock the boat?

A Champion speaks for those who have not yet found their voice.

As a youth I was called a 'big mouth' by my family. I was outspoken and got myself in plenty of trouble. I was told it was wrong, none of my business and to keep my mouth shut.

It wasn't until recently that I realized that Champions speak for those who have not yet found their voice. They stand for their Truth regardless of the results, impact or what others think of them. What about changing your point of view depending on the listener so as to seem amiable? I was doing it right all the time. Society told me I was not so that is what I believed for most of my life.

Do you have an abundance mindset? Or do you hold one of poverty?

Since only one prevails in any given moment, if you have not prepared your mind for abundance, poverty will take the space. One thought or the other; never a vacuum. Do you use the word debt in business or do you use the word investment. Money or revenue generation? Treating yourself as though you are a 'real' business woman, running a 'real' business, begins to develop your mindset of abundance.

Do you have a mentor or a coach or a mastermind? Or do you go it on your own, getting feedback when you need it from anyone who will provide it?

Hold an empty picture frame around your face. From inside that frame you cannot see your whole image. We are all this way. It is a trusted person in your life that sees what you cannot and shares it objectively with you so you get the 'whole picture.'

Occasionally seeking out 'someone' will provide you with a subjective and often judgmental assessment.

Were you (are you) a good follower -- one that surrendered to the leader? Or did you know better, resist and argue with the leader?

If you have never surrendered and followed, as a leader you would be less than effective with followers because you haven't walked in their shoes. It's that simple.

Do you work for a better solution when there are problems? Or do you prefer to be the winner via compromise?

Champions work for Covey's win-win ... a better solution. Here's how this works.

You share an office with another.

You get up and open the window.

Your office mate gets up and closes the window.

You get up and open the window.

Your office mate gets up and closes the window.

A Champion will ask their office mate "why do you keep closing the window?"

The office mate says, "the breeze is ruffling the papers on my desk getting them out of order."

The office mate then says, "why do you keep opening the window?"

The Champion says, "it's stuffy in here; I need fresh air."

The win-win. The Champion walks into the next office and opens that window. You see now there is a breeze and it does not ruffle the papers. This is a 'better solution.' Champions go for the a better solution for all.

Do you step away from a group when the discussion is negative? Or do you find you are sucked-in and walk away feeling low or certainly different?

As a Champion you want to be clear that negative energy and conversation will take you over before you know it. The trick is to learn from the experience. How many times have you come upon a group of people discussing their illnesses? It becomes a feeding frenzy with each person working to 'out do' everyone else in severity of illness.

Richard Brodie in Virus of the Mind shares that negative conversation and energy acts like a virus --moving quickly and spreading thoroughly. A Champion will step away from this conversation. Taking on the negative conversation lowers your amplitude of vibration. Whatever vibration you hold will always match your results.

Take for example the manager who is going for a big promotion. A Champion will 'set the context' and their 'vibration' before entering the promotion meeting. Here's how.

As a Champion walks from car into building and to the meeting, what she is thinking is this: "I deserve this promotion. I have worked tirelessly and proven myself. Management appreciates all I do. They earmarked me when I arrived 2 years ago for this promotion. I am the one who can do the work and do it best." And you are smiling as you are walking and thinking. You now have a spring in your step and your amplitude of vibration is high ... you feel great, confident. You set the context for success.

Not doing this has your default context (negative so often) or vibration to reign. It could mean that you are thinking this as you walk from car to meeting: "I'm not the one they want. I'm sure I messed up. I'll bet there's someone else who is better at this. I'll go anyway and see what happens." You have inadvertently lowered your amplitude of vibration and your results will match it.

Setting the context before the meeting allows you to influence the outcome of the meeting because you are using a universal law (vibration/attraction) to cause or source the outcome. It's not hard to do. You just have to remind yourself to do it.

How do you see failure? As a good thing or no?

Champions know that failure IS learning. It is through our mistakes that we get better. Yet our conditioning as youngsters told us that failure was 'bad.' So we didn't take risks and played small to avoid the limelight.

The Champion embraces failure as did Edison when it is said he tried some 10,000 times to create the incandescent light. Every failure was another way that 'didn't work.' This was good. Ever thought about what it takes to do something ... anything 10,000 times? A whole lot of passion and persistence!

Do you take offense when others use 'certain words?' Or do you immediately find a word that has no trigger so you can focus on what is being said?

Champions are practiced at switching out words so as not to disrupt their listening. First you have to notice that you are triggered. You can tell because you stop listening to the conversation and focus on listening to your inner dialogue. It's saying, this is bad and wrong. Don't they know better?

When I host a seminar or workshop I often use the word Spirit, God or universe. I simply tell participants if they are uncomfortable with one of those, to replace it with the word that resonates with them. Most of them don't notice that they are uncomfortable until I point it out. Knowing allows them to switch out the words.

Do you believe you can be, do or have whatever you want? Or do you believe we are controlled by outside conditions and circumstances and it's only with 'luck' that we are blessed with abundance?

Champions know that we can each be, do or have what we want (part of abundant mindset) as long as you do not violate the rights of others. They've proven it to themselves through trial and error. The reality is that no outside condition and circumstance can stop us for going for what we really want.

Yet we say things like, "it's raining so I won't go walking." A Champion steps up and others step back or look for excuses to not do what is planned.

Here's probably the most important attribute of a Champion ...

When you master this attribute of Championship, you are living your life inside integrity. This is easy to see in business. Not so easy in our personal lives. Here's what I mean.

There is one agreement we humans take together where we include God is marriage. Yet statistics show that more than half of marriages end in divorce and over 75% of 2nd and 3rd marriage end the same way.

First you broke the agreement you made in front of those you love and God. I don't' care why. Just because divorce is now the rule rather than the exception, does not make it okay to break the agreement.

Remember the masses have always been wrong about everything and always will be. No such thing as a Champion with mass mentality.

So then I ask you this. If you are not WILLING to keep THAT agreement intact, why would anyone want to do business with you?

Smart Champions under promise and over deliver. That is when they give their word they make sure they can meet the deadline. They prefer to over deliver (deliver early) in every case.

Champions go one step further by taking full responsibility and then still doing what they promised, the way they promised, with a new deadline. When they do not, they remake and re execute the promise.

Being your Word will distinguish you as a Champion and one of the very few who rise to their full potential.

Do you make quick decisions and rarely if ever change them? Or do you vacillate, asking for the opinions of others and change your mind frequently?

If you have a clear goal you can ask a vital question that will allow you to make smart, quick decisions; the sign of a Champion. **If I do this, will it take me closer to my goal ... or further from it?** If it does not take you toward your goal, don't do it. At least not now. And you can see without a goal, you can't ask the question, so you continue to be distracted by shiny objects that 'look and smell like a good thing' but here you are simply 'playing.'

If you are the person for whom I wrote this book, you are already familiar with a certain lack of 'comfort' when it comes to self assessment. It takes courage taking responsibility for who we are and how we act. It's easier to stay 'outside' with the conditions and circumstances. The truth is this: when you become honest with yourself and ultimately vulnerable and thereby authentic, you are actually FREE. You realize afterward how one simple decision turned out to be easy.

III. Women Wealth & New Ways of Thinking

I.   Navigating the Performance Gap

Only a handful of people actually do what they know to do. Take the best seller Think and Grow Rich. Since 2011 70 million copies of the classic have been sold worldwide. The book synthesizes what successful people do that the unsuccessful people do not ... and have done for 200+ generations. Hill was a reporter who kept up with some 500 citizens that were healthy, happy and wealthy, to find out their secrets. It was Andrew Carnegie that offered the 20 year 'job' to Hill.

Today's most successful people use this plan, whether they have read the book or not. Men have much of this knowledge inherently -- that is it is in their DNA. You only need to watch a man step up to the plate on inner confidence and desire, even though he knows he is not qualified. Women don't do this.

If then, more than 70m copies have been sold and it contains the most concrete plan for expedient success you must ask yourself this question:

Why aren't there 70 million millionaires? Every person that can read can be a millionaire or a billionaire.

Because we "don't do what we already know to do!" And we continue to add more and more information to what we do know -- still not applying what we know.

It's not having knowledge that is power. It is the consistent application of the knowledge over time until it becomes *habilitualized.* That is the POWER.

Take a quick inventory of your books and programs in which you have invested financially and never used. You are not alone. We are invigorated with new information, yet acting on it isn't as invigorating -- it actually takes something.

The difference between knowing and doing is often called the performance gap.

Why don't we do what we already know to do?

We have a slew of beliefs, paradigms, or clusters of 'ways of being' that are automatic. We've believed them as true for so long they've taken hold and we don't even notice them.

The beliefs are based primarily on the beliefs of others ... those we love and admire and whom we want to please. Unfortunately most beliefs of others are of lack and limitation rather than abundance and opportunity. These beliefs have been 'engineered' by default in our subconscious mind or what the Ancient Greeks referred to as our 'heart of hearts.' I will cover how to 'engineer a belief' later.

As children when we 'stubbed our toe' we became more and more careful where we put our toes. It didn't take long to learn that by noon the sand at the beach is so hot you must run to give your feet a chance to cool between strides. We run faster or we wear shoes to protect our tender feet.

Likewise when we are embarrassed or ashamed as children as a result of our behavior, we tend to shy away from repeating that behavior. It's a protection of sorts ... when we are children.

Perhaps your first time in front of the class in early elementary school, sharing a report your wrote, you misunderstood the instructions, reported on the wrong book, and classmates began to laugh and chide you. Fighting back the tears, we plant this truth to protect ourselves, "I'll never get up in front of a group of people to speak again." Maybe that's why some people say that public speaking is a fate worse than death for most!

This protection works well as a child, yet those habits and inner dialogue are 'still running your life.' And as adults this does not serve us very well. We allow ourselves to be stopped from acting on ideas that light us up ... mostly because we don't know how. And the fear of crossing the gap of performance is greater than our desire to have what we want. And we have a host of beliefs that say "it's selfish to want more," or "there simply isn't enough money to go around."

These beliefs keep us playing small and taking no risk. The level of our reward is always the perfect reflection of how much risk we are willing to take.

The process of developing the beliefs of others follows us into adulthood, adding more opinions of others, including television and news reporters. Negativity sells so by default we are 'filled with' the negative points of view of others. When you harness the "power of pause" as you step from 'knowing to doing,' you will see that you always have a minimum of two perspectives or answers to every question.

So it makes perfect sense that when we go to 'step' from knowing to doing, there is a great Fear of the unknown between the two. You want it and you start out, yet when things get dark and you can't see how you can do it, you step back to safety.

Not only are you hearing your own inner dialogue such as "I've tried before and I've failed," or "I'm not smart enough or deserving," or "Someone else is better at this than I am," if you share this with others you will also hear "are you crazy, you've never done that before," or "who do you think you are," or "go get a regular job" (one of my favorites).

It's a battle for the one conscious thought over which you have control over. Why wouldn't you back down if your inner self doesn't believe you can do it and others don't either?

These beliefs are held by both men and women, and for women it is critical that we overcome them. While men automatically step up to the plate in business, women do not. It doesn't matter initially if the man is not competent ... he's first at bat. It's not too long before you realize that just because they 'stepped up' does not mean 'they' will necessarily navigate the gap.

After 45 years in corporate America, my experience is that I more often than not -- and my female counterparts -- ended up more often than not 'finishing up' what they had started!

Why? Because we have been finishing up and cleaning after our families up for more than 200 generations! We're good at it, yet we don't have time to finish up after others *and* still grow our own businesses.

Here's an example. Ready to start, a dozen thoroughbreds are at the starting gate ready for the first race of the season. Behind the row of gates one woman is in charge to get all the horses down the track and cross the finish line.

Three, two, one and the starting gun is fired. As the horses leave the gates, the woman is behind them. Watch her running sideways behind the horses slapping each one as she runs by, saying, "come on boy, you can do it!" Back and forth she runs, egging all the horses on and finally, they all cross the finish line at the same time. We bring everyone across the finish line but no clear star or winner.

Now put a man behind the gates. Three, two, one and the starting gun is fired. As the horses leave the gate, the man is behind them. See him pick out the middle horse and run behind only him, slapping and chiding him to go faster. Finally that one horse crosses the line first and wins the race. He is the star.

Women must learn to practice laser focus on one idea ... and bring it home, to the exclusion of all else. Men already do this naturally. It's not our way. We are the nurturers and peacemakers. Women make sure everyone is a winner. That doesn't work in business.

Navigating the performance gap

When we must step into the gap to apply knowledge and move toward what we want, it is a given that we are afraid. Afraid because we do not know HOW we'll get across. Our experiences have us automatically stop short. If we do not cross the gap we are destined to going to the edge on one idea, shrinking back; going to the edge on another, and shrinking back again.

To solve this problem, I wedged a large coin with a thick edge in the gap. Now you may cross the divide on the edge of the coin.

What value does crossing above the gap provide?

1. You are physically higher than you were before so you have vast vision of both sides of the gap. You see all sides of your obstacle or issue. You see why you shouldn't cross over and why you should cross it, and the best way to do it. You get to make an objective and responsive decision.

2. You have a high level of awareness of your current potential. You can see once you have chosen to proceed the precise steps to the 'doing' side.

3. Even if you 'slip' the edge is wide enough for you to pull your-self back up. Your 'muscle of Faith' is developed enough so that it 'lifts you' back to the coin's edge for a clear view.

4. Decisions that take you from knowing to doing as quickly as possible allow you to grow your business with consistency, momentum and results.

5. Once you are practiced at hopping across whenever you have something new to tackle, you become the Champion for other women who have not found their own 'sea legs' and are in-spired by what you are doing and the results you are getting.

6. You can use this image whenever you know what you want to do and need to do to forward your business, yet are afraid. Every time you lift yourself to the coin's edge, your intellect grows, and soon it becomes a habit.

The Champion has developed Faith ... Faith in herself and Faith in our Universe and how it works.

She lives by the following values from which she avidly seeks their wisdom. These values and laws operate all the time, whether we are aware of them and how they work, or not. Take for example the physical law of gravity. The result of taking a jump off a cliff is well known to all of us. Down we go with an impact that matches the depth of fall and our physical condition. So you don't jump off cliffs.

What if all the principles below also worked all the time and you not only were aware of them, you also studied and applied them in growing your business. You would have an extraordinary advantage and step into the realm of 'the few' who are not only wealthy -- they are healthy and happy. These principles in action spike business growth and momentum and keep it consistent when applied over time. The idea is to have these values become part of you -- automatic, or *habitualized.*

II.   The Power of Pause

Once you begin to step up and cross the performance gap, from knowing to doing, you have a moment at the highest point on the coin, when you are responsive and objective. Only a handful of people even get to the midpoint -- the point where you are the closest to being one with the universe.

You have a big vision of what is possible. In this moment you can stop and be present in the moment. Here you will make clear choices based on what you want. You rise above all the internal dialogue and simply wonder at the universe.

We are so busy as women ... most of us taking on more than any man, because we can and have done so for so long. The importance of being in the moment is critical.

Twice now my women's mastermind group took a sunset boat tour on Jordan Lake late on a Friday afternoon. So consumed with our program goals and building business, we rarely found ourselves reflecting in the power of pause.

While on the lake, I realized there is nothing else to be but present. We couldn't leave unless we wanted to swim! It wasn't long before I found myself mesmerized by the water rushing alongside the boat. I surrendered to the peace. We saw birds atop barren trees in the middle of the lake. We saw bald eagles and blue herons. Pictures, laughter, music, drumming, drink, and food, a large group of Champions peppered the universe with high vibrating energy on those afternoons, reaping same for ourselves.

Practicing pausing when there is a decision to make toward your goals is a practice that will serve you well. You begin by just stopping in the moment and noticing you have done that.

## III.	Belief Engineering.

Belief engineering is exactly that -- engineering or creating new Beliefs.

Why do we need to know how to do this?

1. Our results (bank account, life style, etc.) are *always an exact match to what we believe.* Not what we 'say' we believe but what we really believe, deep down in our *heart of hearts*, the subconscious mind.

2. Whatever you already have matches or reflects what you believe you can achieve and/or deserve. You can be sure that your outer world is a reflection of your belief in yourself and your abilities.

3. With only a handful of people out of each 100 learning how to do this, it gives you the best shot at success at influencing results in your favor.

What is really happening when we 'engineer' a belief?

Use the image to follow the path from when we get an IDEA to the point when we can HOLD IT IN OUR HAND.

1. All ideas are already here and in motion. They start as an IDEA into our CONSCIOUS MIND. We take that IDEA, the spiritual seed, energy that can neither be created nor destroyed ... yet can be CHANGED into other energy forms, and

2. We fall DEEPLY IN LOVE with the idea by thinking about it a lot, writing about it, imagining ourselves already in possession of it, and sharing it only with our mastermind partners.

3. We REVISIT the IMAGE daily and couple it with the emotion of LOVE by adding color and form, smells, sounds, and senses. We do this until this IDEA begins to get very HEAVY and looks to plant itself in our SUBCONSCIOUS mind (heart).

4. When planted, it has its own special EMOTIONAL CHARGE. Because this works fastest by falling in love with an idea we hold OR being in 'hate' with something, the emotion can be POSITIVE or NEGATIVE.

5. Positive emotions partner with a high amplitude of VIBRATION. Negative ones partner with a low amplitude of vibration. Because your MIND is in every cell of your body, your BODY takes on the planted rate of vibration.

6. When you begin to move the RESULTS you get, the ones you hold in your hand, have the SAME VIBRATION as what you believed about it. As you move toward what you want you begin seeing people and opportunities showing up that perfectly match what you want to reach your endpoint.

Sounds simple, right? It's called the transmutation of radiant energy. All you need to know is that in 4 steps you can take an idea (all ideas circulate and if we don't grab onto the ones we get that we love, they wash through us into the next 'waiting' conscious mind) to physical form.

As a child I always wanted to be a magician. How cool would it be to change objects. Now I realize I have always been this. So have you. The power is in distinguishing HOW this process works and then using to 'engineer beliefs that serve us and the world.' These beliefs have a high emotional vibration so our results are joyous.

Universe to Conscious Mind to Subconscious Mind to Form.

Beware: Should you find yourself bored with the idea after a short while (the January to March goal setting example), you must go back to WHY the idea charged you so much in the first place. Bring the image up in your mind and journal a few moments every day or every other day about it as a 'done deal' for a few weeks. Boredom means you didn't spend time 'falling love with the idea' sufficient to have you persist with it. You must be disciplined and consistent. Here is where your trusted mastermind accountability partner will hold you to your word. When we are left to our own devices -- any of us, it takes us longer to reach our goals, assuming you don't give up in the interim.

Good News: Once you have 'planted' the spiritual seed, start watching for, documenting and expressing gratitude for the 'signs' that show up that you once called coincidence. This is a building block of Faith. Faith comes in 3 'waves.' 1) you start to 'expect' things to show up ... it is likely. 2) then you begin to believe you will reach your goal ... you have a firm opinion now. 3) When the seed plants and/or you've had enough proof that it is coming, you have established Faith ... you know that it's coming and it doesn't matter what anyone thinks! YOU KNOW IT. And you know that you know it. Know what I mean?

IV. 17 Principles of Champion Living

1. **Order: The 1st Law of the Universe.** You see the order in our universe via seasons and tides. Can you imagine if we had 5 seconds on Earth with zero gravity? Only 5 seconds starting instantly. Can you see that chaos would ensue? And no promise that order would be restored as it was.

2. **After Order, comes Movement.** Success requires we first have a plan and then follow it. This makes so much sense, yet most of us fire before aiming, then get ready. 'Fire-aim-ready.' No plan? Zero or scant achievement. [There is a great lack of information on goal setting and achievement. For women it is critical as the information is new. Men know it yet it is inherent. I have included eleven comprehensive and critical factors in setting goals that have a high percentage of achievement.]

3. **Out of confusion comes order.** When we learn a new concept that we don't understand right away, we are confused and we have two choices. We can sit with it, look at it, play with it, talk about it ... until eventually it will become clear. You've experienced this with subjects were confusing yet absolutely fascinating to you. When it finally becomes clear, which it ultimately will, you are on a higher level of awareness of your own infinite potential. Choice 2 is to slip back to earlier clarity where we were comfortable. A lesser awareness in our potential is the result.

4. **Repetition in spaced consistent intervals over time is how we learn.** It is through repetition that we learn and our beliefs are formed. It happens all the time ... whether intentional or not. When I learned multiplication tables, we practiced, wrote and recited them every day, not on Mondays only. The tables filled our lives as we studied flash cards and had pop quizzes. The idea was to instill them in our subconscious mind where they would live and be accessible forever. To this day when I am explaining how we learn to any large group, I can give a simple multiplication problem and almost everyone shouts out the answer. Forget the fact that they hadn't done this drill in decades. It is the unintentional or default learning, however, that occurs by default that curtails achievement.

5. **We hold one conscious thought at a time.** Our internal dialogue is not conscious -- it is subconscious. It's the voice that tells you right away when you can't do something or you have done it wrong. The image or picture in our mind in any moment is conscious. Remember when you drove a great distance and lost track of miles? I've scared myself when it has lasted as long as 15 minutes! My automatic (subconscious) behavior (driving) took over and my conscious thoughts were held in focus.

6. **Awareness grows in measure to our learning.** Awareness is a muscle that grows when fed with knowledge ... then applied or exercised. Earning requires learning, followed by practice. Practice becomes a habit and belief; resources rich in wisdom. The more you learn and put into practice as a habit, the harder you are to replace; the more you are able to charge; you become an authority in your field. You can avoid being replaced by never ceasing to learn.

7. **We are gifted with intellect and a body for movement, yet we are first and foremost spiritual beings.** Ideas flow into our con-

scious mind and if they are appealing, we can latch on to them. If not, we let them go and they 'recirculate' and flow into and through another's conscious mind. Choosing to 'hold' the appealing idea because it feels good to you is Intellect. And holding those ideas purposely over time, we bring these 'spiritual seeds,' into physical reality through active pursuit hence, we have a body.

8. **There is no value in what others think of you.** In every case, some will like you and some will not. It's that simple, yet our internal dialogue -- the collection of beliefs that are your truths 'block' access to that reasoning, leaving only ideas of lack or limitation. As your success grows so does the number of people who don't like you ... and those who do. Focus on the ones that do ... there are more than enough to keep you busy for a lifetime.

9. **You can achieve any idea you get.** All ideas are already available. Any idea you get you can achieve or you could say you never get an idea that you cannot achieve. The idea to land on the moon was already here. It came into reality when someone figured out how to do it.

10. **You don't have to know 'how' to do a thing.** With the ability to think only one conscious thought at a time, there is a battle between how to do it and why you want it. How or why is the same battle as the one between faith and fear. A well developed intellect allows us to override our internal dialogue and purposely select the thought that serves our Why the best. When fear shows up, you only need to refocus on your why again to make it vanish.

11. **What we believe matches our results.** Whatever we think about the most -- consistently in repeated intervals over time -- becomes our reality or results. It doesn't matter if we think thoughts on purpose or by default ... whichever ones are pervasive will match our results. If we are caught up in discussions of lack we see more lack. The news in so many forms bombards us with stories that

sell to the masses -- negative ones; the ones that sell. It fills our minds by default and before long we are saying and seeing things that match what we've seen and heard.

12. **There is no value if there is nothing in comparison.** Our truth needs no comparison with the truths of others. This way the truth stands for itself. Comparison dilutes the value of what is so. Yet the masses are always comparing how they look, feel and sound with how others do the same. They make decisions based on another's point of view rather than creating or honoring their own. Because there will always be those who like what you are doing and those who will not, the danger in being concerned with the opinions of others is feeding our own inner dialogue of limiting beliefs. We see slim bodies on television and if ours doesn't look like that our inner dialogue says the same thing. Powerful inner voice and outside conditions and circumstances. The result is a diminishing of confidence, courage and a fading of our authentic voice.

13. **First be it, do it, and then you have it, rather than first have it, then do it, then be it.** When we want something first we find someone who has what we want. We read what they read, follow them, and emulate some of their behaviors. We next take action toward what we want. We have developed a mindset of a person who has already achieved what they want. Then we have what we want. The masses do the opposite. They wait until they have what they want (money) to build something they want (a business), and then they become (be) a business owner.

14. **Great leaders have been great followers.** Until and unless you have surrendered to a leader and followed the rules willingly, at some point in your life, and done it as best as possible, you cannot effectively lead as you do not have personal access to the follow-

er's experience. How would you know their challenges? The follower's experience is vital to the leaders effectiveness.

15. **The Power of Pause (pop).** The power of pause occurs in the middle of the performance gap and allows you to be 100% responsible for your life. A large coin is 'wedged' in the gap so you can go from knowing to doing on its edge, without much fear of falling. When you climb atop the coin you are in a state of objectivity and responsiveness. You see the whole picture and can choose two or more solutions or answers to your current questions. It is a state of presence where you are mentally and physically at the highest level of awareness in the moment. You make your choice and cross the gap to the 'doing.'

16. **Frustration drives improvement.** When we separate what frustrates us from what we see as causing our frustration, we find there is a real need for improvement. The two elements that need to be split apart are 1) our reaction or emotional frustration, and 2) what are the facts ... what's not working. We can then drop the emotion purposely, become objective and responsive, and begin to work on the improvement that is needed. It is said Edison made some 10,000 attempts to succeed in creating the incandescent bulb. What frustration might have driven him? Poor eyesight from reading by candlelight? His eyes hurt which is frustrating. He may have separated the two, let go of the frustration, and jumped head long into the solution.

17. **Mastermind is the Propellant for Achievement.** The universe determines by when and how we get our results -- what we want. Impatient in general, we can step up the process of achievement (success) by refining and clarifying what we want and including others who are focused on your success. The more we focus on the success of others, the more our success grows. This points to the level of investment, matching exactly the measure of our re-

ward. Men have employed mastermind as a feedback to new ideas so long that it's a habit for them. Women however have not yet distinguished business from social as men have, so there is little or no trust between women in business. The practice of looking for the success of another is a vital ingredient to influencing your own success and hurrying the universe along with your requests.

A Special Bonus from Leslie

Now that you have your copy of Champion. 21st Century Women: Guardians of Wealth & Legacy, you are on your way to earning more in business and being a Champion in your life and that of your clients, colleagues, families and friends.

You also receive the special bonus I created to add to your personal and professional growth; something you can use starting today. This journal allows you to study new ways of thinking and apply what you learn, reflect, and note insights about navigating through today's economy as a women doing business in the 21st century.

The perfect complement to Champion, claim your copy here.

http://leslie-flowers.com/ChampionJournal

The sooner you begin learning the things you may not know, the sooner you are on your way to success in business and happiness all around.

Leslie

V.   Women, Wealth & Achievement

Should you be one of the rare 3% (3 of each 100) who couples accurate information for setting goals with the support of a master-mind of like minded individuals (looking for one another's success), you have the formula to achieve what you want as fast as possible. Note that of the 3%, less than 1% is a woman.

What does it take to reach goals fast? The first thing you need to know is to let go of what you know about setting goals -- the things you already know that DO NOT WORK.

To begin, you must know that in our universe, there are two kinds of seeds. This was mentioned previously and is worth talking further about. The physical seed and the spiritual or energetic one which comes in the form of an idea. With physical seeds we can calculate after planting how long with nature's resources it will take for the plant to 'sprout.' We know because we have evidence proven over time.

Spiritual seeds, however, are planted ... yet planted in our mind, where those ideas grow into what we believe. [It doesn't matter if what we believe is true to others ... if it's true for us, it IS our Truth.]

As well it is important to say that each person has their own unique perspective of how the world works. The masses think 'their perception' is the right one. The Champion knows that all perception is true for the individual. Rather than making another wrong, ask them why they believe this and take what resonates with you and build out and grow your own perception on the subject.

When' spiritual seeds' sprout (turn something you want into physical form -- something you can 'hold in your hand'), it all depends on how much you yearn or hunger for it and ultimately your Faith in the idea.

The spiritual seed is governed by a universal law -- the Law of Gestation (germination or gender) -- over which we only have at the very best, certain sometime 'influence.' Understanding the physical and spiritual laws of our world gives us the tools to influence our results or outcome.

Accurate Information

What do any of us really know about setting goals other than a haphazard calculation based on mostly our own misses?

Did we take a class in school or University that outlined the steps of achievement?

When I have asked this question to countless numbers of those hungry for the sense of achievement that we actually are born to experience, I get blank stares.

What DO We Know about Achievement?

Not much. Most people live one year, 90 times over. Sometimes it's referred to as the 'hamster in a wheel' syndrome. You only have to look at the 'health club scenario' to understand this.

It's January and you are at the gym, ready to work out! The room is loaded with equipment and people and there is not one open machine for you. You stand there tapping your foot thinking "I paid good money for this membership and I've got other things to do," perhaps. When a machine does become available you take it.

When you enter the workout room in February, there are quite a few empty machines available. "Good," you think. "I've got to get in and out." And you workout and chat with the neighbor one side of you and then perhaps to the one on the other side of you. Perfect.

March is a different story. The place is empty except for an occasional member here and there. Where is everybody? No one to even talk to.

They've all given up already. Check back the following January and it will all begin again. But will it begin again for YOU? Will you do it differently this time? You can.

What MUST We Know to Achieve Effectively?

What works. We need to know what actually works! Is there an answer out there?

There is one place where it is all outlined very clearly. If you are an aspiring Champion, use the information to plant a bed of achievement, loaded with sprouting spiritual seeds (ideas).

Think and Grow Rich by Napoleon Hill is the precise road map to set and achieve any goal you want, without violating the rights of others. Hill spent 20 years as the 20th century's greatest reporter, synthesizing timeless business principles used since we began recording history -- some 200 generations ago -- to find out what those who are happy, healthy and wealthy (the 3%) were doing ... that everyone else was NOT doing!

It took me five years to figure out why I was immersed in and teaching Hill's classic day and day out. There was a reason. It is because this material is nearly unknown to women, even more rarely applied in business by women, yet it is the tried and true path for business achievement.

Reading the book won't do it for you. It takes study. Yet one of the 13 principles of success in Think and Grow Rich is 'specialized knowledge.' YOU don't have to know everything. You only need to seek out an authority -- someone who does.

That person is often in your own mastermind group. And if they are not, they surely know someone who has what you need.

I'm going to share with you the Ground Rules for Setting Goals you will actually achieve, with predictability and consistency. So you will know. Knowing is not enough, however. It is Guide for setting goals in harmony with universal law and consistent and repeated achievement over time.

You may note that what you think now is in many cases the opposite of the ground rules offered.

Ground Rules for Setting Goals

1. The purpose of a Goal is to motivate you into action. If you are not motivated into action, it's not a good goal.
2. A goal is something you WANT, not something you NEED. Putting food on your table is not a goal; it's a need. If time and money were no issue, what would you leave to the world? Would you open orphanages in the mountains for the underprivileged ... what is it for you? If you could wave a magic wand and you could change the world. What would you do? What do you want to enhance your lifestyle. You are allowed, by the way ... to live in abundance.
3. You must experience some moments of fear when thinking about your achievement of the goal AND more moments when you are completely in love with or obsessed with your goal [the intensity of fear will match the intensity of obsession or desire].
4. Focus on WHY you want to achieve the goal; not on HOW you will do it. It is the 'how will I do this' that stops most people from taking action. We only hold one conscious thought in our mind at a time so if you catch yourself thinking HOW, remind yourself WHY you want to achieve it to begin with.

5. Determine the exact amount of money you need to reach the goal. It's a stab in the dark. It could be a million dollars or more for how you want to make a difference. Set the number. It will scare you and delight you both. You will have to override your inner dialogue which is likely saying "you can't do that," or something like it.

6. Determine the exact date by which you will reach the goal. You are putting the universe on notice that you 'are coming!' and you want what you want to serve. Setting a date allows you to picture by when it is complete which adds to the motivation to take action toward your goal.

7. If you know (or can figure out) all the steps to reach your goal, it is not a good goal. You would have already done it if you knew how. When you only know the first two steps you are forced to continue moving. That's when you will get the next step, and the next, and the next. This is one way we develop Faith. We do it afraid, we do it well, it's not so hard the next time. "There is nothing to fear but fear itself," Winston Churchill.

8. Write out your goals on paper (not digital) and revisit often to add detail. A Harvard study tracked MBA grads who wrote down their goals and when they revisited these grads 20 years later, the results were astonishing. Bottom line to be a Champion you write out your goals and revisit them often, adding color and form to make them more exciting in your mind.

9. Write your goal as though you have already achieved it. Write it in present tense. If you want a home at the beach, imagine yourself walking through the home, smelling the salty air, seeing your family by the fire place or on the beach. Use your five sense to visualize and imagine how great it will be!

10. You do not need one dollar to start toward your goal. If you don't need more than 2 steps, then money is not an issue. Yet "I'll wait

until this comes in, or that happens," are the excuses people use to NOT take action on their goals and dreams. If I want to climb Mt. Everest as an example, I can do two things that cost nothing. Those two things motivate me into action and the next steps come while I am in action. I can research local climbing locations as one step. I can reach out on social media for people who are already climbing. That's it. Not one penny. The forward action immediately sends a message to the universe that I'm on my way to climb!

11. Avoid sharing your goal until your hand is ON the brass ring. Here is where the real "power of mastermind" comes into play, 'causing' results to occur as fast as possible. Back to the spiritual seed. An IDEA when you first get it is new and has no roots. The more you think about it, write about it and dream about it consistently and repeatedly over time, a root begins to grow. This is NOT the time to tell people! Not only will those close to you pooh-pooh the idea (well you've never done it before), your own internal dialogue will be working also to get you to 'let go' of the idea! Your mastermind will support the idea, give you information to enhance it, provide specialized knowledge, and look for what you may have missed to make sure you have your 'best shot' at success.

If we are left to our own devices (not sharing with anyone), and only hear our internal dialogue ... it is made up mostly of "I've never done this before; I'm not smart enough; I tried it and failed; I'll play small and safe -- that works for me," etc.

The 'Miracle" of Chinese Bamboo

I encourage you to watch "The Miracle of Chinese Bamboo." Made a number of years ago by friend and colleague Ginny Dye, it is the perfect segue to a fresh, new way of thinking about ideas and how and how long it takes for them to take physical form. Here is the link to watch it. *http://tinyurl.com/chinesebamboo*

A Word about SMART Goals

When setting a large philanthropic, legacy goal ... one that changes the world, you won't want to use SMART goals. When setting tactical goals in increments to ultimately 'reach' the big goal, you can use SMART goals to manage tasks.

Here's why ...

Specific **(S)**

Measurable **(M)**

Achievable (A) Here's where your spiritual seed will 'die on the vine.' You have no idea how you are going to achieve your big goal and it doesn't matter. If it's achievable we're right back to knowing all the steps, which does not motivate you.

Realistic **(R)** Your big goal when you set it is NOT realistic! Not at all.

Time Bound **(T)**

With two of the elements in direct conflict with the 11 Ground Rules (achievable and realistic), great achievement is not possible.

The auto industry used SMART goals ... great for tactics, not so great for their 'big goal or vision.' In their defense, that was pretty much the only information they had ... so they ran with it. Now we know better. "When you know better you do better," Maya Angelou.

Looking at Achievement in Another Way

Because the way we learn is by reviewing material in consistent spaced intervals over time, it is often important to apply what we know with a new perspective.

Answer the questions True or False and note why you chose the answer you did. Let me know how it goes! You can email me at mailto:Leslie@PathsofChange.com

	True/False
1. Begin setting your goal using your current results.	
2. It's smart to map out all the steps required to achieve your goal.	
3. If you find thinking about your goal scares you, it's a sign to put it away and revisit it another time.	
4. I have a 2004 Chevrolet. I want a brand new 2014 Chevrolet. This is the perfect goal!	
5. As you plan your goal, reserve all funds necessary to reach that goal, no matter how long it takes.	
6. Instead of picking a date when you want to have the goal, focus on HOW you are going to reach it.	
7. Should you find yourself becoming obsessed with your goal, rather than ease off a bit, continue full steam ahead.	
8. Achievable goals can either be something you need or something you want.	
9. Once set, share your goals with anyone who will listen! They become more real this way.	

Learning accurate information about setting achievable goals ... goals that make a difference inside a mastermind group ... is the fastest path to achievement. You start with having the two most vital components for achievement. Accurate knowledge and setting goals that motivate you into action.

You now have a foundation for setting goals that will motivate and excite you and have you living in abundance -- our birthright. Nowhere does it say there is 'virtue in poverty.' Set and achieve your personal goals first and then set your big goal -- your plan to give back double of what you have yourself.

"Until thought is linked with purpose, there is no intelligent accomplishment." -James Allen, As A Man Thinketh

VI. Women, Wealth & Mastermind

Surround yourself with like minded people to create consistent, predictable, and accelerated business growth.

Follow the age-old steps to create a mastermind that provides the specialized knowledge you do not already possess to get your business moving forward quickly.

The age-old steps are the clear achievement outline in Think and Grow Rich, coupled with universal law, with a little quantum and metaphysics thrown in for good measure, and translated into 21st century application for women in business.

Mastermind is the fastest path to success for men and women. All your resources are at hand, saving time as well as money, in your pursuit of your goals.

It is the lack of the principal of mastermind that stands as the single biggest obstacle for women reaching consistent, predictable success in business. Women can do this absolutely. In fact their successes easily exceed those of their male counterparts because their ability to influence results is not inherent ... not yet, that is.

When women came into the work force to feed their families about 30 years ago, they moved from the 'nice to have' income to 'must have' income. I remember my mother in the 50's and 60's working part time for mad or 'pin' money.

The part time jobs turned into full time jobs. Then the two working adult family bought larger homes. Then came divorce and recession and were left with mothers of children living in poverty.

Women were thrown into the workforce with skills that worked at home but not in business. They had no experience and no credibility in that environment.

So how are they making ends meet? They are not ... or are just barely.

What then are women doing wrong? We are making in some cases 17% less than men for doing the same work. What can we do? What don't we know?

The Big Divide

If you look at men's groups such as Lions, Kiwanis and Jaycees as example, these men's groups have lasted for generations. They serve as a business mastermind of sorts -- a place where men bounce ideas off of one another. The key is they *discuss business in one venue and then they have social events at others*. They do not collapse the two.

Women do. We collapse together social and business behaviors and therein lies the problem of developing business momentum with predictability and consistency. There is no trust.

The collapse or the distinction are inherent for women. I've been watching the results explode for women when they have a safe space in which to express themselves and aren't worried about an errant personal attack that could come at any time in most women's groups. It's the group ... it's the level of conscious awareness of the members.

Case in Point. You're new in town and find a woman's group locally. You join. You pay a fee. You begin attending meetings. You have one on ones with others in the group. Time passes and you may even get a referral. Then something happens. One of the women gets nasty and reactive with you and says things that are hurtful. You are uncomfortable and leave the group.

You've lost momentum, time and money.

Not too long after you find another women's group that looks like and smells like it's different ... and the right one for you. You join. You pay a fee. You begin attending meetings. You have one on ones with others in the group. time passes and you may even get a referral. Then something happens. One of the women gets nasty and reactive with someone else in the group and says hurtful things. You don't want any part of this group now and leave the group.

Again, you've lost momentum, time and money.

And it repeats. Any business revenue generation drops like a hot potato. You can't predict now. You are investing money to no end.

Why do women collapse business and social like this? It is because they are unaware of the impact of their behavior. The other piece is there are women who are 'in business for real' and those who are 'playing at' running a business.

Women are nasty with one another. And they are this way in business and in social situations. The key to mastermind is looking for one another's success. Women primarily are looking for one another's failures. They are jealous and conniving and it's a subject most people don't put out on the table.

I know because I was one of those women ... until I learned to be responsive instead of reactive. It took years.

The Champions mastermind focuses on what else is needed for our sisters to become even more great. We know that greatness is a muscle and it is developed in ourselves proportionate to our using it to find greatness in others.

The Champion is not playing at business. They are in business for real. Women's groups have a mix of women playing at business and playing 'for real.'

Everyone is on their own path toward higher awareness. We can however continue learning with others who have the same or similar commitment to lead with a servant's heart.

About playing at business. So many women look at their business as a 'nice to have.' They have another source of income so it is not imperative they generate revenue. And women's groups are full of women playing at business.

The power in this conversation is seeing the collapse of social and business behavior and our ability to separate or distinguish those behaviors. It's new for women.

I've spent thousands of hours watching the power of mastermind live, and in action. I personally have seen mastermind participants develop businesses almost overnight. Easy to do when you can get all your answers through your mastermind group or through one of their associates. And easy also to do when you aren't waiting for a snipe or caustic remark that shakes you to your soul and whittles away at confidence.

Interesting facts about 'mastermind.'

Did you know that Andrew Carnegie (1835-1919) considered the greatest industrialist in the United States attributed his entire fortune to the power accumulated through his mastermind?[4]

Entering the steel business in the 1870's, *"In 1901, he sold the Carnegie Steel Company to banker John Pierpont Morgan for $480 million."*[5]

The personal proceeds he received for the sale of his company was equivalent to about 1 per cent of US GDP at the time. In propor-

---

[4]Hill, Napoleon (1936). Chapter 10, Power of the Master Mind, The Driving Force in J. Ross Cornwell (Ed.) Think and Grow Rich! The Original Version, Restored and Revised. 2007 (177). Chula Vista, CA: Aventine Press.

[5] http://www.history.com/topics/andrew-carnegie

tionate terms that would make Carnegie richer than America's two wealthiest men, Warren Buffett and Bill Gates, combined today.[6]

According to Napoleon Hill, author of *Think and Grow Rich*, the best selling self-help book of all time, mastermind is defined as the *"Coordination of knowledge and effort, in a spirit of harmony, between two or more people, for the attainment of a definite purpose."*[7]

I learned about *Think and Grow Rich* in 2008 and have been facilitating in-depth mastermind studies on Hill's work since that time.

In early 2008, already an avid student and teacher of personal transformation and development for ten years, I landed on the work of Napoleon Hill and *Think and Grow Rich* and began to facilitate face to face weekly mastermind studies of the work.

After facilitating my first dozen multi week masterminds in the first 18 months, I began to notice my own thinking had changed. And I also began to Believe in the principles I was teaching ... from my own results and those of mastermind participants. One thing of which I am absolute sure: **Our results are always the exact reflection of what we believe.** The more I saw proof that these timeless principles work, the more Faith I had in them and the more I could leverage them to influence my own results.

There is no doubt that over the 200 or so generations since recording history, the mastermind concept shows up wherever there is success.

Alexander the Great (Greece 356-323BC) had a group of advisors that by today's terms would be considered a mastermind.

Napoleon Hill, in his classic *Think and Grow Rich* focused on the 'power of mastermind' and refers to it as one of the thirteen key principles of success. Written almost 100 years ago, Andrew Carnegie

---

[6] Thornhill, John (2014) The story of Skibo, Andrew Carnegie's Scottish estate. www.ft.com
[7] Ibid., 176.

commissioned Hill (sans salary), a then 20-year-old reporter, to *repeatedly* interview some 500 our country's greatest successes to find out what they were doing to achieve success ... that everyone else who was not successful *failed* to do.

Think and Grow Rich is the synthesis of timeless business principles when applied in business can handily produce a millionaire. Published in 1937, the 1960 edited version has sold over 100 million copies, making it the most read self-help book of all time.[8]

As you are reading this chapter it may occur to you to wonder *why* — if *Think and Grow Rich* touts the full blueprint for success — aren't there as many millionaires as copies sold?

The answer? Even with the simply stated steps in the classic and with documented, palpable and amazing results over the last 100 years, people still *"do not do what they know to do."*

I would be remiss in excluding Benjamin Franklin in the history of mastermind. In 1727 Franklin created a discussion "Junto" (Spanish for council) based on his 13 Virtues of Living, two centuries *before* Hill wrote *Think and Grow Rich*. Franklin's Mastermind lasted 40 years!

Andrew Carnegie "... attributed his entire fortune to the POWER he accumulated through this 'Master Mind'."[9]

A mastermind alliance speeds up success. You don't have to learn to do everything because likely there is a mastermind participant that has that skill, or knows someone who does. You get to focus on your endpoint, your goal, and not interrupt your flow of work in that direction. This is a new way of thinking.

More and more of us are working alone and we are used to doing everything ourselves. We jump from tasks to grow our businesses (getting clients and other income producing activities) to tasks that

---

[8] The Napoleon Hill Foundation. http://www.naphill.org/
[9] Ibid., 177.

keep our businesses running (managing administrative tasks such as bookkeeping, web site update, etc.). Time is traded and lost ... time that we never get back. We cannot predict our monthly income and the idea of gaining momentum and consistent growth is not even on our radar. It leaves us frustrated and often disillusioned. No one to talk to. No one to trust. No one to share ideas and get feedback. No safe place.

Even when I share with you in this chapter *HOW* to construct and operate your own business mastermind, you likely will do nothing. The performance gap is a phenomenon — knowing what to do and still not doing it. And we even add more and more information to the mix (books, workshops, seminars) ... with which we do little if anything as well.

The paradox is that *being in a fully functioning business master-mind has you break through your performance gap* ... so you actually begin 'doing' what you already know to do, and you put to work new information that comes your way to move you to your desired end-point ... your goal. Amazing.

7 Key BENEFITS of Mastermind

1. <u>Collaborative tasks and talents</u>. By sharing talents with master-mind participants you get to focus on your expertise.
2. <u>Reduce learning curve</u>. Because others are supporting you with their expertise and wisdom, you don't have to trade your time to learn 'everything.'
3. <u>Gain experience, skill, and confidence</u>. Practice gives us experience and skill. Continued successes and business traction builds our confidence in our ability to be a successful business owner.

4. <u>See real visible progress in business.</u> When you are focused on your business goal and not distracted by tasks that 'need doing' that are not your expertise, you can calculate business growth.

5. <u>Instant, valuable support network.</u> You are not sure which company provides the best service. You can pick up the phone or send an email to your mastermind partners and get a trusted instant answer.

6. <u>Consistent accountability system.</u> The best results come from touching base with a 'partner' several times each week. Both people have the goals of the other to assure tasks are being met on time.

7. <u>Develop values of integrity, honesty, and compassion.</u> When you are trusted over time and you do what you say you will do by when you say you will do it, you are developing character and real authenticity.

A business mastermind sounds like a pretty good idea, right? If you are beginning to think about the benefits in your own business you must find a woman's mastermind that splits apart business and social and holds members to high operating standards.

Since early 2008 I have conducted dozens of face to face multi week mastermind studies. Mid 2013 I began working primarily with women and causing this change in women ... that they begin looking automatically for the best in their mastermind partners all the time, not just now and then.

Women absolutely have stepped up into this unique brand of mastermind and the results have been staggering.

Remember for whom I wrote this book. It is for the 21st woman who is a Champion to other women and to their families. She is the guardian of wealth and legacy. She operates by being integrative and being leaders rather than just talking about it. The Champion has experienced success and has confidence and now has a message to share with the world. She grows her business and generates income to expand her message. And the byproduct is more confidence and success.

A Champion mastermind of women is filled with women in business 'for real.' They want you to point them in the right direction and will take it for the most part from there. Of course they need clarification and a helping hand along the way, but by and large, they are self starters who are ready to catapult themselves to success and just need a starting point and a simple map.

To be part of a Champion mastermind you ...

1.	Share a common interest with each participant.
2.	Are committed to the success of all participants.
3.	Have similar skill and/or success level as other members.
4.	Welcome accountability.
5.	Aspire to exceed their goals.
6.	Trust group feedback.
7.	Take action on ideas and innovations from the group.

Success in a mastermind requires that you ...

1. Develop a mission, vision, and/or purpose statement.
2. Set an endpoint goal (large) with monthly milestones.
3. Earmark time each week for the Mastermind.

Let me share a **Case Study** of one mastermind's impact on society so you get the idea of what is possible for you and your business associates.

2009. 8-Week mastermind convened end of summer. Directions were: Stay together. They followed directions.

1. The next year, this mastermind created People-Builders, Inc,
    a 501 (c) (3) non-profit assisting 5 families in getting back on their
    financial feet. They ...
    - built 2 homes for returning veterans with missing limbs or
      severely disabled
    - provided school supplies for children in need
    - fed the homeless on countless occasions
    - supported and hit the Guinness World Record for "most
      food collected in one single event"
    - received the Presidential Citation award for community ser-
      vice.
2. They developed life-long friendships and support group.
3. They are launching a new tech start-up with the goal for being the
    next SAP or Amazon.
4. Together they have shared life changes in marriage and family and
    are now teaching their children the power of love and giving to
    others.

Here's what once was baffling to me. These were all MEN. While most of my mastermind clients up until when I chose to teach women how to win in business using the principles men have used for centuries, were women, and even though I gave all mastermind groups the same instructions -- stay together -- it was only the men who did. Up until recently however. I'm no longer baffled. The source is the lack of safety among women in business.

I am still inspired by what this group is doing and it made me even more focused on finding out what it actually takes for women to 'stick together' in the same way.

Napoleon Hill .... the man who really brought the word 'mastermind' into our everyday vocabulary, states in *Think and Grow Rich,* "*No two minds ever come together without, thereby, creating a third, invisible, intangible force which may be likened to a third mind."*[10]

My personal goal is to cause the collapse of wage gap by 2025 rather than 2054 when statistically expected, by providing women with vital missing business information and how to apply it the fastest way possible.

In 2013 I realized what was missing for women the presence of which would give them a gigantic leap toward earning more.

MASTERMIND
Key Requirement for Achievement

1. Knowledge
2. Trust
3. Connection
4. Momentum
5. Consistency
6. Predictability
7. RESULTS

In addition to the guidelines Napoleon Hill outlines so perfectly in Think and Grow Rich, it has become clear through long experience in mastermind facilitation, that these 7 elements pictured — from knowledge to results — are the 'railing' to hold while moving toward achievement.

Note that Trust is the second element -- the biggest challenge for women in business. We do not trust each other.

---

[10] Ibid., 176.

First you **learn** in an environment of **trust** and **connect** which set business in motion, gaining **momentum** with **consistency** and **predictability** over time. The **RESULTS** have been staggering for women.

Anatomy of a Women's High Performance Mastermind Model

There are 8 essentials required in building a results oriented women's mastermind that will serve as the foundation for success in business and in life. The model builds Champions. Champions who know their purpose and are on a mission to bring it into form.

Women doing business and living inside this model for the last year or more have experienced growth in business alongside women who have promised to only look for the greatness in one another -- and they kept their word. They are Champions. They can do this because they know that both greatness and fault are available by law and that we get to choose what we think.

These women know that their own greatness grows in exact measure to their finding it in others. They know that *"I am the mirror of your greatness; and you are the mirror of mine."* They've practiced *being* Champions in spaced repetitive intervals over time until they are now becoming *habitualized.*

10-Week Cycles

I have found that 10-week cycles (quarterly and rolling) work the best for setting tactical steps toward business building and legacy building. I have also found that while women do not stick together routinely, when they choose to step inside this foundation for business and living, they excel, succeed and are very happy doing it. A hidden benefit is the lifelong power partnerships that are built on trust.

The cycles allow achievement of an intention that grows business and seeds of future programs. Because women do not typically stay with one group as I have explained, they don't get the chance to actually 'build' consistently. They may get a jump start yet it quickly loses steam because there is no solid structure for growth.

We take on a lot as I have mentioned because we are good at it, while men focus on one thing. We bring in the whole team, they bring in one member. They shine.

Once we offload all the goals we start with, save one, we are clear and we begin to move.

What happens to the things that were offloaded? And what about when seeds of business already planted start showing up? How do we stay on course?

The 10-week mastermind allows seeding of future cycles and intentions, of course. The obstacle there is choosing which goal to reach for next. 10-Weeks seems the perfect time to bite off a business goal and achieve it or better. This grows the business and confidence of success in business. We have to have lots of successes to build the level of confidence held by our male counterpart. The most meaningful piece is the power to influence your own results once you have seen for yourself the power of learning and mastermind, first hand. It is proof of Faith. Yet even with all that proof, it is natural to question ourselves. It is because we never really get rid of old beliefs, we simply over write, or outweigh them.

A clinical professional in this high performance mastermind, who had an idea to transform her industry thought about it for 5 years. In her first 10 week mastermind experience, she documented her idea in a workbook and held a paying workshop. Fifteen weeks later she had tripled her annual income using her new concept.

A financial professional found at the end of April this year she had already reached the measure of all last year and was on track to exceed 300% growth this year.

A strategic marketing professional became a best seller twice in one month during one 10 week program.

These are women who already knew confidence and success, had found their message -- purpose and passion — and wanted to grow their businesses to expand their reach. They are moving down the road and do not want to stop. They do need some directives along the way.

They know that someone is waiting for these women building legacy to speak ... for those who have not yet found their voice. To be the Champion in the lives of those they know, and soon will know.

I have also found that the 10 mastermind sessions are peppered at specific intervals with the same information provided from a different perspective. Stretching the muscle of perception is vital as the way things look change in measure to our level of continued learning.

The pieces women need most ... goal setting and confidence through results ... show up right off the bat and continue throughout the program. The weekly journal follows along with each teaching module with room to note insights in preparation for the Q&A calls.

We write in long hand when we journal. Writing gives us enough time to think. And because the only thing human beings have control over is what we think. We may influence others with what we have learned, but that's it. We know that outside conditions and circumstances are meaningless when in pursuit of your goal, mission, passion, purpose or dream. We call them different things, yet it's what motivates us into action that counts after all.

The content refers often to the principles of success in Think and Grow Rich, along with universal law, emotional intelligence, transformation, coaching ... the coming together of 20 years in personal development ... into the most comprehensive mastermind program I have been witness to.

Women have found a home with other women, without fear. It has to be developed like a muscle, however, because our nature is being challenged. We aren't in tune to business success, yet we bring vital skills to the table in business. Right now business leaders for the most part don't listen to women, and not by intention. Imagine if women were listened to ... what would happen to the top and bottom line of any business. Better to have the skills of both men and women at the conference table rather than that of men and women 'sitting in.'

It's easy to see that setting goals and confidence show up early and often when reviewed and repeated. The content of each module is rich in principle, law, intelligence, value and virtue. It is a foundation that has life make sense. Women need this as they have been thrown into business without a life vest.

Accountability is clear cut as women have shared one of their biggest challenges is staying focused. No surprise as we naturally do tasks in tandem. It works when managing a household and family. It doesn't work in business. Women must sharpen their ability to focus on doing what they say, the way they said they would do it, and by when they agreed to do it.

In the first high performance mastermind, participants speak from 30-60 minutes twice a week with a partner, and one 30 minutes call a week with a program mentor (been through 2 or more cycles). How to conduct the accountability call is outlined and includes simple coaching questions. What did you intend to do. Did you do it. If not, why? What will you do next? And so on.

In the second and future cycles of this high performance mastermind program, accountability partners speak 5 days a week for 30 minutes. What begins to happen is the development of power partnerships among accountability partners and the birth of new businesses. These are the hidden gifts in mastermind. You don't expect this to happen because remember, women don't trust each other and are so often unkind.

Foundational agreements include the promises of the mastermind. It includes how to do business with one another with integrity. As example, we want to have a one on one to learn about one another's services. At the end of that meeting a clear decision is made whether you will do official business with the person now, or later. We are very careful to not take advantage of the strong skills that are right at our fingertips.

A list of primary and secondary skills and areas of expertise of mastermind partners are available so it's easy to go 'close' first.

A lot of time is spent on the subject of Faith, which is no real surprise. Even after covering the subject, step by step as to how to build Faith on purpose, our nature and old inner dialogue still has us question what we know. It becomes less and less and our intellectual 'muscles' at this point are strong enough to 'hush' the inner dialogue.

While we understand intellectually the process of building Faith and pure belief that what we want, we will have, it's another thing to internalize it. Considerable time is spent first identifying and then developing a deep yearning for our large philanthropic goal and then the incremental steps we take in each mastermind cycle toward that end, growing our business along the way.

It is clear that throughout time achievement was based first a clear picture of what we want and then developing a hunger and yearning to have that thing. When we begin to buckle in the face of 'not knowing how' or 'I've never done this before,' it is the power partners that become the hand rails to steady this sister until she can stand on her own again.

Two inner dialogues.

One of the most powerful skills women operating inside this model is the ability to distinguish the two inner dialogues we hear.

I say two because one is your own cacophony of primarily negative and limiting beliefs that tend to keep you playing small or safe in business and in life.

The other is the voice of God or the Universe. Let's agree that there is one universal force of energy of which we are all a part. If we can do that you can call that entity whatever you like. That is also a powerful skill. Because we only hold one conscious thought in our mind at a time, if we are learning and a word, like this case in point, has a negative associated emotion from an incident when you were a child, IT pops into your mind. While it is there, you are MISSING what is being said. You can't have concurrent conscious thoughts. Even a computer, fast as it goes, still does one thing at a time.

Our inner dialogue from beliefs which reside in our subconscious mind and are hidden from view are filled with emotion.

The voice of the universe is heard via imagination in our conscious mind -- imagination being one of those mental muscles, and the 5th principle of success in Think and Grow Rich.

You can distinguish the two voices over time by authentic journaling. Sit down the same time every day in a place that feels comfortable to you and begin journaling in a notebook ... ask questions. Do not stop or hesitate; just write. First you will hear your own internal dialogue answering and in a short time you will notice a different tone when you get an answer.

The two sides of the conversation are faith and fear, devil and angel -- same as inner subconscious dialogue and conscious conversation. We hear both voices in our conscious mind.

Here are examples of results. Some happened in one 10-week program, some in two and some in three.

1. Time: 8 Weeks
Intention: 50 Qualified Leads
Result: 125 Qualified Leads

2. Time: 10 Weeks
Intention: Workbook and 8 week course
Result: Workbook and Paying Workshop

3. Time: 20 Weeks
Intention: Coaching Certification
Result: Certificate Award

4. Time: 10 Weeks
Intention: Present Paying Workshop
Result: Presented 2 Paying Workshops

5. Time: 3 Weeks
Intention: Develop and Test Program
Result: Program Live with 12 Paid Participants

6. Time: 10 Weeks
Intention: Build Web Site and Develop Marketing Materials
Result: Web Live, Materials Complete

7. Time: 4 Weeks
Intention: Double Monthly Income
Result: Income Doubled

8. Time: 30 Weeks
Intention: Leap in Business
Result: Annual Income Tripled

High Performance Mastermind Model

The Model includes **Essentials for ...**

- ★ Personal and Professional Integrity
- ★ Setting Intentions and Getting Them
- ★ Building Confidence
- ★ Accountability and Mastermind
- ★ Developing Habits and Beliefs
- ★ Self Assessment
- ★ Influencing Your Outcome
- ★ The Power of Completion

In this image, WE are the juggler, happy in general, moving across the 'tightrope' of life.

The Safety Net

The critical elements for success starts with the Safety Net. We walk the tightrope of life and we will fall and fail. The Champion knows that failure is how we learn.

Who is holding your net right now? Is anyone? Can you count on all 6 of those holding the net, or is it haphazard and often you slide to the ground rather than bounce back?

The net is held by the women you can Trust, who look for your greatness only, who will catch you every time, women you can count on.

Next is Learning. As we learn, apply, *habitualize*, and grow in awareness of our true potential, the weave of the net thickens and becomes more buoyant. The thickness and buoyancy grows in direct measure to the amount of learning we take on.

These images are filled with content throughout the mastermind program.

When we aren't being judgmental and catty, conniving and unkind with one another, and stay focused on conducting 'real' business and our success, we are even more powerful than men. I realize all women are not this way. The challenge is the varying levels of awareness of this behavior and the absolute requirement for IT TO CHANGE. I watch women I've known for years gravitate from one women's organization to another. It all seems to be working until we get nasty with each other.

One bad apple can spoil the barrel ... an old expression, yes. A mastermind alliance cannot work with even one bad apple. Think about one of the oldest alliances in history ... that of Jesus Christ. I don't have to tell you what happened in that mastermind with only one bad apple seated at the table.

Men have inherent or habitual ways of doing business successfully yet they do not leverage those ways because they are simply unaware of the power of their habits. No awareness provides no leverage or influence. When women learn to separate business from social, they wield full power by consciously influencing their own outcome.

Women are stepping up to the plate like you every day. You must take on the role of Champion and be the role model that will lead western women into powerful positions of influence.

It is your responsibility. I will tell you that if you know your message ... or are very close to knowing ... there are thousands waiting to hear your message. And they are waiting to hear it from YOU. You could say it is selfish to NOT share your message ... and/or to not search desperately for it.

Most people realize their purpose and see the 'big picture' on their death bed. You cannot Champion others when you are dead.

The mastermind I have developed requires a list of promises and commitments agreed to by clients ... with one being ONLY looking for one another's success. Life changes when you have habitualized the search for one another's greatness and success potential.

It takes some practice. I don't know about you, I like playing the game and never really liked the 'practice' part. Practice in tandem with highly evolved and intelligent women actually makes the practice fun.

Imagine if you could see momentum growing in your business and predict and count on an accelerated income generation? You don't have to imagine any more. I've spent twenty years bringing together the best of the best transformational programs and concepts, mixed them up and peppered them with my own theories, with resulting business burst and personal growth for all, based strictly on your level of engagement.

VII. Conclusion

The problem? Slow traction, growth, and income increase for women in business. Expected date of closing of wage gap estimated mid century.

The solution? A high performance women's mastermind that is tried and true, vetted and practiced, a foundation of learning and integrity, with measurable results over time.

How to? You can apply the principles in this book to design your own mastermind if you wish to invest the time and inclination. Or you can join one that is in existence.

Results, by when? Results come in small increments. Noticing each and every success, regardless of size, will prove to you that it is your new way of thinking that causes your new results. What you generate will be a direct match for your investment of time, passion, and money. You could start now!

This book was designed for the Champion woman to achieve while living a life she loves. First there is clarity (we operate best when clear) and then one explanation about why we aren't earning what we deserve and have worked for, so we get that the state of our financial affairs are "not our fault."

We took a look at we are as business women in the scheme of things; where we are, where we want to go and how to get there.

My intention is that the woman for whom I wrote this book steps up and out and embraces higher awareness with other in kind women.

VIII.　　10 Selected Studies

If you are a Champion for whom this book is not enough, I have included several teaching pieces to further grow and enhance your awareness of your true potential. The more you learn and apply, the broader your potential appears to you. One day it will be infinite.

1.　　Your Bank Account Matches your Beliefs
A lesson in cybernetics.

Shut the door, you're letting in the cold air."
You know how your air conditioning works, right?
You set the temperature of choice, which is maintained.
Someone leaves the door open midsummer.
The temperature begins to rise.
At a point, a message is sent to the unit.
Message says 'start cooling.'
Cooling sustained until original set point is met.
Upon reaching original temperature, message to unit says stop.
This is a demonstration of a cybernetic system.

"I'm leaving on a jet plane "
Here's another … auto pilot.
Flight plan entered from Chicago to London
Flight takes off, reaches cruising altitude, auto pilot switched on
Over the Atlantic there is a fierce storm.
The aircraft is thrown off course for several minutes.
Storm subsides (or pilot flies above or below it).

Autopilot takes over again and you are right on course.

Hello Heathrow!

Johnny 'believes' he is a C student.."

Here's another … high school student.

Johnny has always been an average student.

Cs and C+s throughout elementary and middle school.

Johnny's parents want him to go to college, but Cs aren't the way.

They inspire, motivate, and even commission him to study harder and do better.

Johnny's inspired all right! He works feverishly over the next weeks.

His grades rise on the next report card. His parents are elated.

Alas, after a few weeks elapse, he is no longer motivated and slips back into C-dom.

Now you are likely pondering … how … and what in the world does my bank account have to do with keeping my home cool, getting to London from Chicago, or Johnny's average grades?

All three examples factor into your current bank balance. They are all cybernetic systems. The first two are pretty obvious. The third is a bit tricky and is the KEY to your REVENUE GENERATION!

Let's look at Johnny. Could have BEEN you, could BE you, and could be your Son or your Grandson.

The set point or automatic pilot is WHAT for Johnny? If you said "the automatic or habitual way of being," you were spot on! All Johnny's life his grades reflected that he is average. His teachers refer to him that way, as do his parents. The other children know him that way. HE BELIEVES HE IS A C STUDENT! And why wouldn't he? That's all he has heard from those he loves and respects all his life.

He'll never out-perform being a C student …. Unless … unless what? If you guessed "set a NEW set point," you were right! It absolutely can be done!

So then, look at your lifestyle and bank account to start. IF nothing could stop your dreams, are they where you want them to be? Keep in mind one must generate DOUBLE what is needed for self sustenance to honor the law of reciprocity (so you get to KEEP it).

If you said yes, I would ask you to reconsider. If you said no, I will tell you HOW you can begin to develop NEW BELIEFS in your ability that ABSOLUTELY WILL MATCH your bank account and lifestyle.

2. The Outspoken Child
I was called a 'big mouth'

Were you an outspoken child?

Was yours the first hand raised, ready to risk giving the wrong answer, so you could be first?

Did parents or teachers frequently ask you to "please just shut up?"

Did you always have something to say on any subject?

Were you then 'shut down' by adults and authority figures, making you feel you weren't being heard?

Did you FINALLY BELIEVE that you had nothing to say that anyone wanted to hear?

If any of these questions WERE YOU … now ask yourself this one …

Do you still BELIEVE these things? Likely you do. I do.

I am the epitome of that child. And it wasn't until recently that I learned that I DID HAVE SOMETHING TO SAY, that I say it well, from a place of courage and wisdom, and that I SPEAK FOR THOSE WHO HAVE NOT FOUND THEIR VOICE!

I was almost 60 years old when I learned and took 'to heart' that those things I was told and believed about myself, MAY NOT BE TRUE … not NOW. [And it is likely they never were true.] So as a child often we are rebuked as a protective mechanism or make decisions to not take risks so we are not embarrassed in front of other children.

Now at 65, considered an expert in personal development after 15 solid years of study and application, there are those who have decided they don't want to learn from me. They are adults and have their own internal conversation and perceptions born as a child who has them judge me and others based on beliefs of their parents and loved ones.

Now I am faced with peers who don't care what I know or what I offer. They are more interested in making me wrong, gossiping and being jealous – than learning what they DON'T KNOW to grow themselves and even more important, to SERVE THEIR CLIENTS. It amazes me. Those I call on the carpet for being unprofessional, out of integrity, and gossips – your gossips with a reactive and low level of conscious awareness of people's greatness, DON'T LIKE IT ONE BIT.

I learned long ago that "what other people think of me is none of my business," and assuming I'm not violating anyone's rights or any universal law. We know of the law of polarity which is that there is ALWAYS good and evil present; no up without a down, etc. So there will always be those who appreciate you – and those who do not. So as long as I speak my Truth, I no longer care about those who are not all about learning what they don't know and being of exemplary service to others. It is my hope that one day they will be. Unfortunately most people as another mentor of mine, Les Brown, says … most people 'get it' … but on their death bed.

I am doing what I love! Teaching people the things they didn't know to live into full abundance starting right now, our birth-right, or things they knew but need to hear again from another voice because they have grown so much since they heard it the first time. Hundreds have improved their joy in living this life when studying with me and THAT is my passion.

For those who were always quiet and the observer children … you KNEW ME as I spoke the things you didn't say while I took the heat. Either way, it's time to speak your Truth, guard the wealth and our legacy, and lead others to a higher awareness of our inborn infinite potential.

3.   imagine unimagined wealth

Since man began keeping written records some 6000 years ago, records were kept by men, used by men, written for men, and kept secret from women. Men did business and practiced universal truths, laws, principles, and virtues until eventually those practices became habitual. While men operated businesses outside the home, women, operated inside the home.

The 1970s -- when women began to take work outside of the home and women's lib was on the scene -- it seemed that this action was likely at least part of the source of the massive breakdown of western marriage. Divorce rates 40 years later for first marriages are at 50% and much higher for 2nd and 3rd marriages. Why is this important?

With marriages and families splitting apart, mature adult male role models were also disappearing. Now male adolescents had no role models to emulate! Just 75 years ago, families ran businesses together, communities spent time on projects – so there were plenty of adult men around. Today most young men don't even have a father as a role model, let alone uncles, community members, church members, etc. What that means is that when men hit mid life and their own fear of dying, they revert back to adolescent behavior, and mature women woke up one day married for a long time to a teen-aged boy!

Even with the lack of male business role models, the habitual use of business tools articulated for centuries is now inherent and automatic for men, with or without role models, somewhat like the 100th Monkey Syndrome. They have had the advantage in the business world without even knowing it.

Women are now deeply steeped in the business world – they are not just now entering it. Yet they come to this world without the business skills and tools that are already automatic for men. Women do have emotional intelligence skills from their centuries managing home and family, but those are not the business skills required to 'get ahead' in the business world and generate unimagined wealth.

Women don't just want to earn the $.23 for each dollar that men do. They want more! The challenge is that because nearly all great works were written by men and for men, they may not resonate with women. More and more men are going home to manage family as more women are out in the business world so it is imperative women learn these skills, or remain behind men in pay earned, even for performing the same work.

The translation of these male oriented documented works into a woman's point of view goes a long way in having women gain these skills with alacrity, and collapse and EXCEED the pay gap in very short order. Men who learn these business skills – or distinguish them intentionally – have a bigger advantage than women with those skills.

Refer back to chapter 1 where reveal those 3 simple business secrets so that women can enjoy unbridled and unimagined wealth... and so that the smart men that choose to learn and revisit them on purpose, will watch their revenue catapult exponentially. Wealth is ours for the taking. Few enjoy it due to this missing information. In the end it's learning that is the miracle grow for human beings.

4.   Doing things 'afraid'

Everything sounds perfect... except for one thing, she said.

"I'm AFRAID!"

"Yes," I said, "I know. Did you know that really successful people look at 'being afraid' as a BIG GREEN LIGHT to grow? We muster courage when we are afraid and when we DO IT ANYWAY, we grow in awareness of our REAL and infinite potential!"

She did it... AFRAID! That was my daughter when given an opportunity for which she had prayed and asked for two years.

A 16 year middle school science teacher, twice nationally certified, recent teacher of the year, and now coaching middle school teachers, my daughter started seeing herself stuck in one job until retirement and she was not happy about that visual. [Many would be thrilled to have that kind of tenure, right?] She is well liked, well known, and well respected in her position, yet under normal teaching curricula; she was unable (like any teacher) to teach only advanced children or her favorite subjects, in depth.

She was offered a position to 'create' a science curriculum for advance students in 6, 7, and 8th grades for an entire county. But it would mean changing schools!

She was comfortable at her old school. She knew the curriculum, the teachers, the students and the administration. And they all knew her.

This would be a new school, a new curriculum to develop, new administration, teachers, and logistics. Nothing to count on except, if this new curriculum were done well, SHE would be the ONE to teach it to other science teachers all over the county? How perfect this answer to her dilemma!

After our talk as you saw above, she made the Decision (8th principle of success) and took the job. While she mentions to me that as students matriculate out of middle school, they always come back to see her and she would miss seeing them, hey, she says out loud, she could put a picture of herself on her old classroom door with her new location so those kids would find her.

Remember this... when you 'feel' uncomfortable, there are on-ly 2 ways to go...

Your comfort zone where you grow very little (if at all) and of which you may not be inspired, motivated or even fond.

Out of your comfort zone where you muster courage, stretch, and grow into your own greatness.

Next time something you really want shows up and it scares you... will you do it 'afraid?'

5.   On Faith ... Show Me Some Proof

I remember being frustrated when I heard people say "just have faith." Okay, I thought. How do you do that? Just have faith? For inside the word 'just,' lies a whole bunch of things to do and think about to 'cause' this thing called faith. Faith in ourselves, our God, and our universe.

Faith is acquired in 3 simple steps. They are simple and yet you may already know that just because something is simple does NOT mean people do what they know to do! That's emotional intelligence and discipline wrapped up into one.

When we source faith in anything, the first step is it being 'likely' to or we expect it to happen. Then as we think about it, imagine ourselves in or around 'it,' consistently over time, we learn to have a 'firm opinion' that it will happen. And finally, exercising step 2 repeatedly has us BELIEVE it is ours. Nothing can change our mind. That's pure faith. That message when sent to the Universe, returns precisely what we believe.

Here's proof in a fun case study I've written for you so you can see that what we want and think about, positive or negative, is already on its way toward us. If we settle for anything less, what we wanted is then diverted or circulated to the 'next' person who wants it. Keep in mind we must be expecting what we want and most often NOT from typical sources.

As Thoreau said, ""If one advances confidently in the direction of his dreams, and endeavors to live the life which he has imagined, he will meet with success UNEXPECTED in common hours."

Already aware gal pal called for a short coaching conversation. She had worked for months tirelessly and in love with a new company that would yield her over $200k in commissions in those few short months. You'd be working tirelessly too!

Then out of the blue, she was fired. She never got anything in writing because she trusted the company and of course she did not get $.01 of the $200k due her. Yes, she did earn it all. You've been here... if she had the money to litigate, she wouldn't need to litigate.

So her story, mantra, or the thing she said to herself repeatedly was "I'll never see a dime of the money I earned from that company!"

When I heard that I knew what needed to be done to be sure she DID get the money... but not from THAT company, from an unexpected source!

Focusing on that mantra had her unable to even consider looking elsewhere for remuneration.

On the call I suggested she change that mantra and every time she caught herself saying "I'll never see a dime of the money I earned at that company," she would now say, "I will receive all the money I have earned, yet it will come from another source." And so she did.

Three days later she sent me a note that she had to talk with me right away. That the mantra 'had worked!' She had been very intentional about changing this 'mantra,' and guess what?

Here's the rest of the story.

Seems someone she knew mentioned an mlm outfit... my friend thought "I signed up for that 18 months ago but I never did anything with it." She called the person who enrolled her and to her surprise, he said, "where have you been? You have $1m in product in one leg! All you have to do is 40% of the work to earn big time (and a car) from this company!

The lesson here is this: Taking her focus OFF 'never getting paid' and putting focus on 'I will be paid' AND 'watching for it in unexpected sources,' proved that what she had earned faithfully was already sitting and waiting for her, but not from the original, expected source!

6.   On Getting "Un Stuck"

What are you DOING to apply the knowledge you already have? How often have you given up on your dreams? And for what seems at the time, very good reasons?

Are you feeling stuck?

When we move into our internal journey of life... when we don't blame outside people, conditions, and circumstances... is when we notice those dreams never did die... they are still there... albeit just a little sprout or glimmer of what might have been.

Most of us begin the inner journey somewhere around mid life, however, many never get it, even on their death bed. They've spent their entire life like a hamster in a wheel, trying different things and the same things consistently to get what is wanted. They never get it. Yet with these 4 components on any journey, you CAN DO IT! And, in record time!

1. Start with an end point. Make it something you can 'fall in love with' -- something you really want -- not something you need. Without have a defined point to which you are moving, you remain a hamster in the wheel.

2. BE the change. Take on the characteristics, ways of writing and thinking, clothing, travel... anything and everything you can do to already be 'being' that person. Find someone doing just what you dream of doing and being. Watch them closely. Living as though you have already reached your end point is required to reach it without giving up.

3. Walk through fear. No matter the obstacle, cavern or mountain, cross it or climb it. If you are nervous or don't want to... all the more reason to do it! Courage shows up when we do things that we fear yet will absolutely move us forward toward our dreams.

4. Lean toward the end point. Heads down on your path, letting no one interrupt you, if you lean well over, you must move your feet toward the end point. Not moving your feet has you stumble which is how we learn, so get up! Your dream is just over the next hill.

7.   Applying the Knowledge you Have

While intellectually we know we are born with infinite potential ... well almost.

Then you know what happens... the perspectives of those we love become our own beliefs until we reach the age of reason and then they still do, but we at the very least at six we can begin to 'reason' things out for ourselves.

You also know by now that what we truly believe we can accomplish, we will. So saying I will be a millionaire, or half millionaire, or CEO... is meaningless UNLESS we believe we can do these things.

I have found that even with the best knowledge (we have a bunch of that), without adjusting or reshaping new beliefs that serve us (the old ones do not) and/or without taking action toward what we want, what we want is meaningless without Faith in our own abilities.

Setting a goal that is absolutely lovable and very much wanted and thought about a lot is the 'how' we grow in awareness of our abilities. Goals provide the incentive for us to learn and grow in awareness. As we move toward our goal, we are faced with obstacles always. It is our love, persistence, desire and clear image of what we want that has us break through those obstacles and come out on the other side, even closer to understanding we CAN execute any idea we are given.

"I am grateful to the idea that has used me." Alfred Adler, Psychologist

Taking classes, online courses, workshops, and seminars ad nauseam is simply packing in more information. My question is after you take one of these trainings do you set appointments during the week for several months on your calendar to review and apply the information? This causes a habit, a new belief in your ability. If you are not doing this then I would suspect that you results – getting what you want – do not match your desire.

This cannot be done now and then, by the way. Think about the multiplication tables we learned in elementary school. We didn't just practice them every Monday alone, did we? We did this daily or every other day with consistency over time. Bless our school systems as I doubt they understood what they were doing... just that it worked. And today, those tables have carved 'cells of recognition' in our brain so that if I ask you today what is 6 x 7 you likely 'automatically' respond 42. The tables are habits.

While we only hold one conscious thought at a time, the more things we can turn into a habit, the better. That way we can take on creating more and more habits consciously that lead to excellent and desired results.

Now it's TIME to start applying the information into our life in spaced consistent intervals over time. Then we will develop perfect Faith in our own ability to reach our potential.

8.   Exploring Intellect?

We all have intelligence. It's one of our two gifts as spiritual beings. The other is our body, the means by which we take ideas (spiritual seeds) and move them with desire and persistence into physical form.

Our intellect is a group of mental 'muscles' that when well developed, allow us to over ride our lifelong conditioning and/or the opinions of others. Like any muscle, if it is not intentionally and actively used, it withers and atrophies, leaving us to take action based on outside conditions and circumstances (over which we have zero control) or on the survival techniques developed as children (old beliefs), which served us then, but by no means serve us one iota... now.

Because the first law of our universe is Order, and out of confusion comes order, it makes sense that we must be very clear in understanding how mental muscles work and how to develop them to take charge of our thoughts so we stay aligned with what it is we want.

Only human beings have conscious awareness and intellect. While many would bet a week's commission on their 'dog' having a conscious mind and awareness and they can prove it! Take the bet. A dog 'knows he is in the room with you," but unlike you, he does not 'know that he knows it.'

Where are these mental muscles, and what do they do? Even if you are acquainted with them already, because we learn via repetition and because you are now more aware than you were when you first (if at all) came in contact with them, they bear repeating.

They are perception, intuition, imagination, memory, reason and will.

These muscles, intellectual faculties or spiritual warriors (my favorite term for them) reside in the conscious mind where you can consciously accept OR reject any idea, whether it comes from another person or outside information, or from within based on our beliefs about how life works. It's important because in our conscious mind, we are only able to 'hold' one thought at a time.

Example: You are driving home from work and you get the 'perfect' idea for a new process that will boost the ROI of your company right away! And then... out of the blue, someone nearly side-swipes you! If you have not developed your mental muscles sufficiently, the bright idea leaves your mind and now it's filled with the 'near side-swipe!' That idea is gone now.

Had your 'spiritual warriors' been developed over time to manage your conscious mind, you would have had enough control to 'hold' that image, regardless of what's going on as you drive.

Why hold the thought? Well, it is the thoughts we hold consistently and repeatedly over time that move from the conscious mind into the subconscious mind where they "live like the truth." They are now a 'belief' of yours that is hidden from your view, has you act habitually around it, and they cannot be rejected.

Example: While driving to my new home just 4 months after moving in, I got into a heated discussion with my ex husband. Having lived in an apartment a distance away the 4 years prior, my automatic conditioning stepped in as my conscious mind was 'heated!' Guess what? I drove through the gates of my old apartment complex! Some 20 minutes away! Because my conscious mind was very involved with the 'conversation,' my automatic conditioning or habits 'took me home.' But living in a new home for 4 months after an apartment for 4 years, had the 'apartment' habit take over.

Perception: How you view the world. Perceptions always changes -- when we get new information. Everyone has their own 'unique' view of the world. My way is right and so is yours. Remembering this and practicing it will have you avoid proving the point that 'your way is right.' All ways are right. Then real conversation and synergy can occur.

Intuition: This muscle is our connection with Source (God, Spirit, Universe). You recognize it when you 'know' you shouldn't, do anyway and then say, 'I knew I shouldn't have done that.' It's a feeling or guidance, rather than an emotional reaction. Reactions come from the subconscious; intuition speaks into the conscious mind and guides us to be in harmony with our innate brilliance.

Imagination: Pretty well programmed OUT of us in elementary schools as we daydreamed and heard the teacher say "Joey, quit daydreaming and pay attention to the lesson!" Imagination is the workshop of the mind and is required to bring an idea to physical manifestation.

Memory: Often I will hear people say things repeatedly like "I always forget to do this," or "I'm getting older so I'm more forgetful." This could not be further from the truth. We each have a perfect memory, however, if we tell ourselves this repeatedly and over time, we begin to believe it as it has 'lodged' in our subconscious mind as a 'habit' or belief.

Reason: When undeveloped, any muscle, and particularly 'reason' works against us and what we want. So if you get a wonderful new idea and you are excited about it and you keep it to yourself to preclude others from trying to change your mind, a past belief will likely pop up from your belief system and say something like, "you've never done that before," or "you're not smart enough to pull that off," etc. And an under developed reason, rather than saying "wait a minute, thanks for sharing, but we're moving forward with this idea," it will say "right, you'd better give it up so you won't fail or embarrass yourself.

Laser Focus: Because many of us have ascribed to the concept of "multi-tasking." Multi-tasking is not only impossible (even fast computers really do only one thing at a time) but it diminishes our ability to focus on one idea.

9.   One good idea

Bill Gates started tinkering in his garage decades ago. And… he did not STOP, based on any outside conditions and circumstances (money, time, other people's opinions). He puts his pants on one leg at a time just like you and me. Once, even he was making ends meet, dreaming, and moving forward with his idea, not knowing what would come next. Average looking, didn't dress well, Bill was just your average Joe with a dream.

JUST LIKE YOU… AND JUST LIKE ME.

We are never given an idea that we cannot execute.
If you can think it, you CAN DO IT!
Gates had his moments of fear I'm sure. Even with all he has earned, note that he is acutely aware that giving back and living a life

filled with value and integrity is required to maintain success.

Look at numerous political figures with plenty of money and opportunity. Yet they made choices that compromised integrity and values and ultimately, their true nature was discovered. We can only hide the truth about ourselves for 'so long.' We know when someone is walking the walk.

No matter what, keep on keeping on! Find like minded people who won't try to stop you! They are around, you just have to look. The naysayers and those who see the glass as half empty are stronger in numbers and have had plenty of practice 'being' naysayers. What is most interesting is that they really believe their perspective is the truth. It is... for them only. What they do not know is that the glass is also half full AT THE SAME TIME it is half empty. We simply get to CHOOSE what we think. That is our gift as human beings. And what we think provides our results all the time, every time.

We cannot solve today's problems with the same kind of 'thinking' it took to create them (paraphrase Einstein). Go and get new knowledge needed to take the next step and beware of getting caught in the cycle of taking classes. Time must be earmarked to apply that knowledge into our everyday life. It takes both: knowing AND doing. Investing in knowledge is only half the picture. Without action, those dreams go back into the universal 'collection' and on to the next person... the person who will hopefully ACT on that idea.

Those who are successful in all areas of life are NO DIFFERENT THAN YOU ARE... Except for one thing... They KEEP MOVING, regardless of circumstances.

Often as we move toward what we want, we are faced with our own questions, such as

It's taking too long.

It's not working.

I've invested enough.

My friends say I'm crazy.

And our own inner voice reminds us of our failures and to not take risks; to play it safe. And 97% of people give up on their dreams and quit. Often they are just a few steps toward WILD success.

Now what about YOU? And your DREAMS? Will they accompany you to your final resting place because you were afraid, didn't know how, thought someone might steal them, didn't have enough time and money?

OR will you step out on Faith, find like minded people, learn what you need to move forward... And then MOVE? Fear is pretty tiny once you step into its FACE.

10.   goal setting—before you start

Goal setting is my favorite area of mastery. Watching people plot out their lives and unleash their imagination is inspiring. Once you begin to follow these simple rules you will have the best shot at success!

Since only a few folks are really successful "across the board" (all areas of life) you might find it noteworthy that only 15% of folks set goals and less than 5% write them down.

So it's obvious that setting goals and writing them down gives you a 'leg up' toward your own success.

Here are 9 Musts for goal setting (and achieving). This is what you need to begin your new year business plan and now you have this extra 'edge' and incentive to make this coming year the best year ever.

1. Do not set a goal based on your past results. Those results were achieved before you learned these steps; old thinking. It takes the same energy to, as example, make $50k per year as it does to make $60k. Starting with old results would be making $50k/year and setting a goal for $60k.

2. Do not set a goal where you already know all the steps to achieve it. You would have already done it and you haven't.

3. The goal should be so large that you FALL IN LOVE with it. When we desire or want it very, very much, we begin to believe in it quickly when we are 'in love'.

4. The goal should be so large that you are uncomfortable with it or even afraid. If it's easy, we don't do it. When we step through our fears and do it anyway, we begin to see more of our infinite potential. Fear or discomfort are a BIG GREEN LIGHT for the successful because they are getting ready to grow!

5. Be specific about how much money you want AND by what date you will achieve it. Our birthright is Abundance -- there is plenty to go around. Our job is to make ourselves comfortable and we must have a goal that far exceeds what we want for our own comfort. Why? Because by law you must then GIVE BACK. Those who make a lot of money and do not give back -- ultimately LOSE IT.

6. Determine 1 or 2 small steps toward that goal and START RIGHT NOW, regardless of circumstances. It is when we are in 'action' that all the other steps are revealed to us through ideas we get or people we meet.

7. Do not focus on HOW you will achieve the goal, but rather WHY you want it. The WHY will have you focus on falling in LOVE

with the goal; the HOW will stop you -- "I don't know how to do that," or "how am I going to get the money to do that."

8. Have the goal serve your overall purpose. We all have the same purpose ultimately; that is to serve others. We may not know the vehicle for the service. If we don't then a large exciting financial goal will get you comfortable, have you live abundantly, and your vehicle for purpose will show up during the process.

9. Share your goal only with like minded, supportive people. A goal is an idea and is a seed or sorts, which takes time to root and grow into your BELIEF THAT YOU CAN DO IT! If you share it with others who begin to question it, you may find yourself throwing it out as you have second guessed yourself.

IX. What Clients Have to Say

YOU NEVER GIVE UP! That would be an apt subtitle for Leslie Thomas Flowers's newest work – Champion. 21st Century Women: Guardians of Wealth & Legacy.

Leslie has achieved something extraordinary with this book. She has taken the up and down events and circumstances of her life and produced from them a road map, a step-by-step blueprint for today's women struggling to achieve success in business and in life.

J. Ross Cornwell, Editor/Annotator
Think and Grow Rich!: The Original Version, Restored and Revised, first editor-in-chief of "Think & Grow Rich Newsletter," published for the Napoleon Hill Foundation.

As an active member of Leslie's Think and Grow Rich masterminds and 4 of her women's mastermind groups, I must say her work is life changing! It is amazing the depth of self awareness and personal growth that comes from learning from a master. Leslie receives my highest recommendation for her knowledge of success principles, her ability to take complex concepts and share them in a practical way we can all understand, and caring for her clients.

Diana Needham
Marketing Strategist | Online Media Strategist | LinkedIn for Business | Best-Selling Author | Speaker

Leslie Flowers has really created a masterpiece here in *CHAMPION 21st Century Women Guardians of Wealth & Legacy* that I personally have recommended to even my teenage daughters to read. As a successful Online Marketing Strategist and entrepreneurial woman, I had read Napoleon Hill's *Think and Grow Rich* several times but until I read Leslie's book and got into her top Mavenz Mastermind Program I realized that I had just read the book not actually mastered it and I was definitely not using the concepts strategically in my businesses.

The idea of being a Champion is one that really hit home for me as an entrepreneur and particularly as a woman and mother raising four daughters. I want to be a Champion for myself and as a role model. Leslie sets into play exactly what you need in a step by step easy to follow methodology that anyone willing to take disciplined action can follow. For me, I have become laser focused and have used Leslie's feminine interpretations of Napoleon Hill's work to completely rework my business model to literally "add a zero" to my financial bottom-line this year. You can do this too!

With Leslie's personal stories of struggle and her underlying message to never give up makes her very relatable and clearly positions her as every Entrepreneurial Woman's Champion and is a MUST READ if you are ready to Game Up in your life or business with a proven strategy for success!

Thank you Leslie! You are a true Champion!

Tina Williams
TinaWilliamsConsultingGroup.com

Leslie Flowers is an extraordinary mentor, leader and educator. She has an innate and remarkable ability to take complex concepts and present them in a simple and usable format. I have benefitted personally and professionally from my participation in her Think and Grow Rich for Women series over this past year, achieving results quickly and easily. I would recommend her program to any female entrepreneur who is interested in gaining personal success while maintaining a high level of integrity, professionalism and class.

Peggy Norwood Stella, M.A.
Exercise Physiologist, Creator of A New BMI, Health Coach

With Leslie's mastermind program for women, my life has gone from pretty "dark" to total "light and happiness". My results continue to move me toward my most passionate life goals. She is inspiring to say the least. Her program provides the structure and accountability so that you DO get results. Through the law of repetition, she shows us how to put Napoleon Hill's "Think and Grow Rich" into actionable steps, in order to grow our business so that we can give back IN A BIG WAY to the community or world at large. Thank you Leslie for all that you do! Please join her program, it is THE best investment, and THE best value out there. You need try no other program.

Lisa Carl
Clinical Trial Management and Project Management

I don't know if she realizes this, but Leslie Flowers has played a major role in my personal and professional transformation over the last year. I've watched her from afar at networking events, read her blog posts and engaging discussions on various social media sites. Last December I attended my first Leslie Flower's workshop and much of the information she was sharing was relatively new to me. I attended my second Leslie Flower's event in April of this year and I was once again blown away by the vast amount of information she provided along with engaging, eye-opening activities. Even though a portion of the information shared was similar to the first workshop I attended, I had GROWN so much in those few short months that I heard her speak to me in a totally new, even more transformative way. Not only does Leslie simply share information, she does a phenomenal job of making sure you understand, know and become aware of how the concepts she teaches is showing up in your own life and business. Since taking Leslie's workshops I've gone from a struggling business owner with a multitude of self-limiting beliefs holding me and my business hostage to stepping into my power, raising my level of consciousness and nearly doubling my income. All I had to do was consistently implement what she teaches and I immediately began seeing tangible results. I will certainly continue to learn from this Master Teacher.

Megan J. Huber
Business and Life Success Coach

Workshops

A MUST ATTEND event (workshop) for women who want to close the gap between what they earn and what they should be earning. Personal growth expert Leslie Flowers won't disappoint in her amazing workshops.

Olalah Njenga
Marketing Consulting and Management
President, YellowWood Group

Leslie has been my coach during the critical start-up phase of my content marketing and publishing business. In just one goal-setting session with her, I identified 10 new revenue channels and prioritized next steps to tap the ones that inspire me the most.

She's like Miracle-Gro for business development; I could do it by myself, but my efforts are more fruitful when I add her insights. She coaches me on the fly, preparing me for critical conversations with clients. As I play out my business on the court, she's on the sidelines ready to show me when, why and how to improve my game.

Working with Leslie is the best decision I've made since starting my business. And as it grows, she'll no doubt play a key role in my continued success. I highly recommend her services to those looking to spark innovation, growth or revenue generation for individuals and teams at any stage of the game, from start-up to enterprise

Nanette George
Founder & Storyteller at Bright Publish

I hired Leslie to facilitate a Goal Setting workshop for a group of my Team Nimbus clients. Leslie did an amazing job creating a powerful and effective experience. She provided us the principles and knowledge and then facilitated our use of that in creating really great goals for 2011.

She connected quickly with the group; gave us a robust goal setting framework and led us to create an inspiring and focused set of goals.

Leslie is excellent to work with and I am seeking additional ways to benefit from her skills and expertise.

Bill Davis
Owner, Team Nimbus of North Carolina

Believe~2~Succeed Seminars for Women in Business

I've had enough of "same-old, same-old". I KNEW I had to move into this unknown space to find myself and my purpose.
Deborah

I was amazed at how like-minded all of the women in the room were -- yet this w as the first time I had met many of them! I feel that by connecting with these w omen, I will be able to see more clearly the direction in which I need to continue, as they w ill see and hear things in me that I don't see and hear in myself.
Raye

People need a safe environment where they can express fears and at the same time get real solutions so you can move forward. Leslie provides that space and has the know ledge to take you forward.
Kathy

I entered the seminar with the intention of regaining my power by reconnecting with my intuition. The content of the seminar completely restored my faith in my own Inner Wisdom, as well as promised me tools with which to solidify that experience into daily practice.
Rangadevi

At the seminar, I felt a deep connection with Leslie's message success and abundance as I am fearful of change and the unknown. Leslie says, "Do it anyway. Do it scared." It was as if I had been waiting to hear those words in order to move forward in many areas of my life, especially entrepreneurship.
Chrystal

Leslie is extremely motivating and encouraging! She clearly
knows her stuff. Being with so many accomplished and
motivated w omen w as very empowering and energizing!
Dori

I felt vulnerable and scared attending Leslie's seminar but knew
that I needed to get clarity. I learned that w e all have different
road blocks and that there is no right/wrong, better/worse
when it comes to those things that which w e struggle with
daily. Having a safe environment of other like w omen has been
a source of strength for me!
Kate

X.　About the Author

Leslie Flowers is an author, presenter and advisor who empowers women to tap their genuine inspiration, plan for success and achieve their fullest potential. She works with female entrepreneurs, team leaders and executives to identify values build high-performance teams, reach consensus on strategy and more.

As a young woman, Leslie lived in San Francisco and served as a flight attendant during the Vietnam War. At 30,000 feet, she hosted troops flying from the United States into war zones and back.

She spent 45 years working for businesses from lean start-up to corporate enterprise. There, she grew her skills in writing, production and publishing. Her attention to detail and quality earned her executive respect as a trustworthy brand steward. Her direction of a proposal and production team for one small business won a $30 million contract that put the company on the map.

Leslie developed her core leadership strengths during 20 years of immersion in multiple transformational techniques for personal growth and positive change. A key influence on her work was Napoleon Hill, author of the timeless best-selling book on personal success, Think and Grow Rich!, originally released in 1937.

"Leslie and I have discussed Napoleon Hill's life and work extensively. This lady knows what she is talking about."

-J. Ross Cornwell, editor of Think and Grow Rich! The Original Version Restored and Revised and first editor-in-chief of Think & Grow Rich Newsletter, a Napoleon Hill Foundation publication.

Leslie started her own business to show others how to come "face to face with their infinite potential." Since 2008, she has facilitated more than 35 in-person "mastermind" studies on the principles of success and goal achievement for hundreds. Each 10-week study trains participants to tap their interests, pursue their passions and achieve their personal goals. Participants have used her training to start their own businesses, write and sell best-selling books and more.

"The most important take-away from my work with mastermind participants is that even when we know what it takes to succeed and we understand it, we rarely take the steps necessary to achieve it," says Leslie. "We start by identifying barriers to success so we can transform them, accelerate achievement and consistently achieve high performance."

Leslie is mother of two children and grandmother of four. She loves to entertain guests in her dream home on a lake, a vision she held for five years and brought into reality through her work. She enjoys spending time with her grandchildren and has a passion for empowering others to develop success skills and achieve their greatest potential.

For more information, visit Leslie Flowers on **LinkedIn** or on her **website**, www.leslie-flowers.com.

A Special Bonus from Leslie

Now that you have your copy of Champion. 21st Century Women: Guardians of Wealth & Legacy, you are on your way to earning more in business and being a Champion in your life and that of your clients, colleagues, families and friends.

You also receive the special bonus I created to add to your personal and professional growth; something you can use starting today. This journal allows you to study new ways of thinking and apply what you learn, reflect, and note insights about navigating through today's economy as a women doing business in the 21st century.

The perfect complement to Champion, claim your copy here.

http://leslie-flowers.com/ChampionJournal

The sooner you begin learning the things you may not know, the sooner you are on your way to success in business and happiness all around.

Leslie

XI. Insights and Inspirations JOURNAL

As you read this book you will have insights and inspiration which you may wish to capture in the following pages.

THESE ARE IMPORTANT and critical to your growth in awareness of your true potential.

Note on each page of reflections, the chapter and page so you can refer back with ease.

When we are inspired and we write it down, we are more likely to revisit those ideas and move into action on them.

"Writing causes thinking; thinking creates an image; images control feelings; feelings cause actions, and actions create results."

— Leland Val Van de Wall, on the learning process.

Insights and Inspiration #1

*Chapter:*_______________________________________ *Page* _____

Insights and Inspiration #2

*Chapter:*___________________________________ *Page* _____

Insights and Inspiration #3

*Chapter:*_______________________________________ *Page* _____

Insights and Inspiration #4

*Chapter:*_______________________________________ *Page* ______

*Chapter:*_______________________________________ *Page* ______

Insights and Inspiration #5

Insights and Inspiration #6

*Chapter:*_______________________________________ *Page* _____

*Chapter:*____ *Page* _____

Insights and Inspiration #2

*Chapter:*____ *Page* ______

Insights and Inspiration #5

*Chapter:*____ *Page* _______

Insights and Inspiration #6

*Chapter:*____ *Page* ______

Insights and Inspiration #7

*Chapter:*____ *Page* ______

Insights and Inspiration #8

*Chapter:*____ *Page* _____

Insights and Inspiration #9

*Chapter:*____ *Page* ______

Insights and Inspiration #10

*Chapter:*____ *Page* _____

*Chapter:*____ *Page* _____

Insights and Inspiration #11

*Chapter:*_______________________________________ *Page* _____

Insights and Inspiration #12

*Chapter:*___________________________________ *Page* _____

Insights and Inspiration #13

*Chapter:*____ *Page* _____

*Chapter:*____ *Page* _____

Insights and Inspiration #14

*Chapter:*____ *Page* _____

Insights and Inspiration #15

*Chapter:*_______________________________________ *Page* _____

Insights and Inspiration #16

Insights and Inspiration #17

Insights and Inspiration #18

*Chapter:*_______________________________________ *Page* _____

Insights and Inspiration #19

Chapter: ____ *Page* _______

Insights and Inspiration #20

*Chapter:*_______________________________________ *Page* ______

Printed in Dunstable, United Kingdom